BROADWAY THEATRES

History & Architecture

William Morrison

Dover Publications, Inc.

Mineola, New York

Author's Acknowledgements

Photographs, drawings, and other materials for this book came from many sources. The author wishes to express his thanks to the following for their invaluable assistance in the compilation of these materials: Catha Rambusch of the Rambusch Decorating Company; Jeanne Newlin and the staff of the Harvard University Theatre Collection; Melissa Miller-Quinlan of the Humanities Research Center, University of Texas at Austin; Mary Ison of the Prints and Photographs Division, Library of Congress; Kathryn Mets and Marty Jacobs of the Theatre Collection at the Museum of the City of New York; Laird Ogden of the Prints & Photographs Collection at the New-York Historical Society; Anthony Robins, Jay Shockley, and Marjorie Pearson of the New York City Landmarks Preservation Commission; Seymour Durst of the Old York Foundation; Bob Taylor and the staff of the Billy Rose Theatre Collection, New York Public Library; Dr. Brooks McNamara, Maryann Chach, Regan Fletcher, and Mark Swartz of the Shubert Archive; Mr. Marcy Chanin; Bernard Crystal of the Joseph Urban Collection at Columbia University; Christa Mahar of Hardy Holzman Pfeiffer Associates; Raymond Wemblinger of the Hampden-Booth Theatre Collection at the Players Club; Peter and Peggy Elson for access to architect Herbert J. Krapp's drawings and photographs; Preston J. Kaufman at the B'hend-Kaufman Archives; the Wisconsin Center for Theatre Research; Fox & Fowle, Architects; Bill Benedict of the Theatre Historical Society of America; the staff of the Photographs Collection of the New York Public Library; photographer Lionel Freedman; Irvin R. Glazer; Michael Miller; Craig Morrison; and artist Mark Hylton. For their reproduction of historic materials and photographs, the author would also like to thank the Leigh Photographic Group of Princeton, NJ, the Princeton University Photographic Service, Only Black & White of Charlotte, NC, and Authenticolor, Inc., of New York City. Individual photo credits are listed page 168.

Published in Canada by General Publishing Company, Ltd., 30 Lesmill Road, Don Mills, Toronto, Ontario.

Bibliographical Note
    Broadway Theatres: History and Architecture is a new work, first published by Dover Publications, Inc., in 1999.

Book designed by Lisa L. Cangemi

Library of Congress Cataloging-in-Publication Data

Morrison, William (William Alan)
    Broadway theatres : history and architecture / William Morrison.
        p.   cm.
    Includes index.
    ISBN 0-486-40244-4 (pbk.)
    1. Theaters—New York (State)—New York—History. 2. Performing arts—New York (State)—New York—History—20th century. 3. Performing arts—New York (State)—New York—History—19th century. 4. Theater architecture—New York (State)—New York.
I. Title.
PN2277.N5M58   1999
792'.09747'1—dc21
                                                                99-14611
                                                                CIP

Manufactured in the United States of America
Dover Publications, Inc.
31 East 2nd Street
Mineola, N.Y. 11501

Introduction

Bright Light Zone, Great White Way, Crossroads of the World, America's Main Street . . . these are but a few of the extravagant names that have been applied to the Times Square Theatre District over the years. At its peak, during the Roaring Twenties, Broadway's multitude of playhouses, opera houses, movie palaces, concert halls, and theatres in the area could accommodate more than 160,000 patrons on a single evening.

The first major theatres in the district were built on Broadway south of 42nd Street. Showplaces like the Casino, Empire, and Broadway—and the Metropolitan Opera House—were packing them in during the Gay Nineties and after. Then the impresario Oscar Hammerstein built his huge Olympia and Victoria theatrical palaces north of 42nd Street, the New York Times moved into its new headquarters, and Longacre Square was renamed Times Square. Within a few years this rundown part of the city became its premier amusement center. In 1916 New York's zoning czars made it official, designating the area as an entertainment zone.

A variety of factors converged to recreate Times Square as one of the world's great theatre districts: The three most important were the city's population, which doubled to almost 2 million between 1870 and 1900; America's amazing prosperity, which not only created millionaires but also provided a good living to a growing middle class; and the arrival of the nickel-fare subway, which brought thousands of people to the area every night.

Just after the turn of the century there was a major theatre building boom. Around 1900 an average of ninety new productions were housed in some twenty-three theatres; in 1918, 135 shows were housed in fifty theatres; and by the late 1920s a seasonal average of 247 new productions were divided among some seventy-six houses. Successful shows ran longer and stronger. Once unheard of, 500 performances were now well within reach, and a handful of smash hits topped 1000. At a time when producing costs ran about $10,000 for a straight play and $40-$50,000 for a musical, some shows had revenues in the millions. A hit could bring in $2000 for every dollar invested. Showmen and speculators flocked to the stage, even though there were still far more failures than successes, especially for the unwary.

Another significant factor in the Broadway building boom was the rivalry between two would-be monopolists: the Theatrical Syndicate and the Shubert Brothers. Though each side worried that there were too many theatres on Broadway, neither wanted to give up the race to the top. Even after the Shuberts won, they continued to build, and by 1927 they controlled forty-three theatres on and off Times Square. A.L. Erlanger, sole survivor of the once-mighty Syndicate, controlled a mere fifteen. But then Wall Street laid an egg on October 29, 1929, as the famous headline in the show-business newspaper *Variety* said, and the Depression that followed hurt Broadway badly. The Shuberts and others were forced to file for bankruptcy. Business slowly improved, then took a dramatic leap forward during World War II and its boom aftermath. Since then, the New York theatre community has been through many more ups and downs.

As Broadway moves toward the 21st century, the number of active theatres hovers around thirty-three. During the 1997-98 season, thirty-two new productions opened, and attendance climbed to 11.3 million people. The mega-hit shows, running for years and thousands of performances, can occupy up to ten of the theatres, but many of the other houses continue to have problems. The New Amsterdam and New Victory theatres, magnificently restored, reopened during the 1990s. In addition, the Ford Center for the Performing Arts was the first new playhouse since the Marquis opened in 1986. Along with a renewed Times Square, Broadway began to boom during the 1990s. But while the future of the big new office buildings in the area seems assured,

Introduction

occupied as they are by Conde Nast, Reuters, and other media power-houses, the future of the legitimate theatre is always in doubt. The granting of landmark status by New York City to the exteriors and interiors of most remaining houses may play a part in slowing the rate of attrition. Nevertheless, many observers have concluded that the number of active theatres will continue to decline, if not through demolition, then by conversion to other uses. (Off-Broadway continues to thrive, operating in smaller, less expensive houses that operate under different conditions and union rules.)

The theatres described and illustrated in this book span over a century of change and innovation. The long, narrow auditoriums of the 19th century gave way to open spaces with shallow, fan-shaped seating plans. Multitiered horseshoe balconies supported by view-obstructing posts evolved into the single deep balcony supported by cantilevers. The plain storefront entrances of the 1800s were replaced by ornate and ostentatious facades owing more to the Beaux Arts and other European traditions than to the plain American model. Then, as the ornate became more expensive and less in fashion, most streetfronts were decorated only sparsely. Auditoriums were generally built parallel to the street rather than straight back, to provide more space for audience and stage.

With the complex problems of how to provide good sight lines and acoustics, how to integrate modern technical equipment into existing theatres, how to comply with ever-more-restrictive building and fire codes, the legitimate theatre has presented difficult design problems to the architect. Small wonder, then, that most theatres have been designed by specialists. In the mid-to-late 19th century the field was dominated by John Bailey McElfatrick (1829-1906) and his large firm. Francis Hatch Kimball (1845-1919) came down from New England in 1879 and, among other achievements, pioneered the use of fireproof terra-cotta in theatres and other buildings. The firm of Henry Beaumont Herts (1871-1933) and Hugh Tallant (1869-1952) had a hand in many of the great playhouses after 1900, including the New Amsterdam and Lyceum. George Keister (1863-1945) designed the Stuyvesant, Selwyn, and Earl Carroll theatres, among others. For about five years (1909-1913) William Albert Swasey (1864-1940) was principal architect for the Shuberts. The most prolific theatre specialist of the 20th century was Thomas White Lamb (1871-1942), who designed over 300 vaudeville and movie palaces. His legitimate theatres included the Cort, Candler, and Hollywood (a movie house that became the Hellinger).

Herbert John Krapp (1886-1973) was associated in one way or another with the Shuberts from 1913 until well into the 1960s. He built dozens of theatres in the Broadway area quickly, economically, and with inventiveness and taste. A good many of his playhouses are still in service. The designers and architects of today's theatres are often specialists in restoration or in the development of arts centers. Among the premier names on Broadway are Hugh Hardy, the firm of Beyer Blinder Belle, and Roger Morgan Studios.

This book does not pretend to be a comprehensive, academically oriented survey of the theatres designed by these and other architects. It is offered as a pleasant, informative stroll through the New York theatre district, hitting most of the high spots, omitting some others for reasons of space. The shows mentioned as opening at each theatre are by no means offered as a comprehensive list—merely as an attempt to catalog some of the productions that have been most successful, most enduring, or most interesting as the work of a noted playwright or composer.

Table of Contents

The seventy-four theatres are listed by their original names, even if the name lasted only a short time.
Under each theatre are all important subsequent names, with the dates of the name change, and dates of demolition.

Table of Contents

Fifth Avenue Theatre

27-31 West 28th Street

Stephen Decatur Hatch, Architect • Opened December 3, 1873; 1529 seats

The old original Fifth Avenue Theatre was on West 24th Street, adjacent to the famous Fifth Avenue Hotel. It was called the Fifth Avenue Opera House until 1868, when Augustin Daly took over as manager and began booking first-class plays. Among his successful productions was the controversial drama *Divorce*, which ran for 200 performances in 1871–72. Like many gaslit theatres of the day, the Fifth Avenue burned down, January 1, 1873. The family that owned the nearby Gilsey Hotel offered to keep Daly's company in the neighborhood by remodeling the old Apollo Hall, on West 28th Street just east of Broadway. Daly accepted their terms, and the new Fifth Avenue opened its doors before the year was out. Among the early attractions were appearances by such celebrated performers as Edwin Booth, Eleanora Duse, and Lily Langtry. Despite these successes, Daly did not fare well financially, and in 1877 he left to manage his own Daly's Theatre. The Fifth Avenue continued under a succession of managers to offer popular entertainment, including the American premieres of Gilbert & Sullivan's *The Pirates of Penzance* (1879) and Offenbach's great *Tales*

2 The rebuilt 28th Street facade, Fifth Avenue Theatre, 1892

of Hoffmann (1882). In 1891 this Fifth Avenue was also destroyed by fire, undaunted the Gilseys decided to rebuild. Architect Francis Hatch Kimball moved the main entrance to Broadway but designed a striking facade for the 28th Street portico, where balcony and family circle patrons entered. He also incorporated in the new building such late-19th-century innovations as fireproof construction and electric lighting while improving audience sight lines by keeping the number of balcony-supporting posts to a minimum. The only trouble with the new playhouse was its location: The theatre district was moving north, toward Long Acre (now Times) Square. Although the newest Fifth Avenue was acclaimed for its comfort and beauty and attracted first-class productions—Minnie Maddern Fiske starred in *Tess of the D'Urbervilles* (1897), *Hedda Gabler* (1898), and *Becky Sharpe* (1899)—in 1900 the building was leased to F. F. Proctor for his vaudeville shows. Silent films were added to the bill around 1915, and after the Crash of 1929 the Fifth Avenue became a burlesque house. In 1939 the old theatre was razed to make way for an office building.

1 The Fifth Avenue Theatre of 1873-91 had an unremarkable but dignified Italianate brownstone facade enlivened by gaslight standards on the marquee and along the second-floor balustrade. Atop the buildings was a pediment displaying the theatre name and supporting a statue of the Greek god of music and verse, Apollo, playing his lyre. *(Photo on previous page.)*

2 The new brick walls for the 1891 rebuilding of the 28th Street lobby and facade were faced with terracotta profusely molded in a dizzying variety of caryatids, garlands, panels, pilasters, window surrounds, and stringcourses. Fire escapes were artfully placed to provide an unobtrusive emergency exit through a neighboring building.

3 The 1891 auditorium decor followed the Renaissance precedent set by the exterior. Its ornate plasterwork was finished in ivory with drapes of crimson and gold trim. The house ran back from Broadway, parallel to 28th Street, allowing greater width than was possible in the 1873 building. There were individual seats for all patrons—benches were old-fashioned now.

4 The lobbies of the renovated Fifth Avenue Theatre were paved in white marble and decorated with colorful rugs, draperies, and other furnishings. Paired ionic columns and pilasters added to the classic elegance, and mirrored walls below the ornate vaulted ceiling gave the illusion of grand size.

3 Auditorium toward house right, Fifth Avenue Theatre, c. 1900

4 Lobby, 28th Street entrance, Fifth Avenue Theatre, c. 1900

The Casino

1404-10 Broadway & 120-30 West 39th Street

Kimball & Wisedall, Architects • Opened October 21, 1882; 875 seats

One of the great landmarks of New York's theatrical world, The Casino was for nearly five decades the city's leading temple of light opera and operetta. This highly wrought Moorish fantasy, built for the Vienna-born composer/producer Rudolph Aronson, was partially modeled on the Newport millionaires' playland of the same name. Yet it was in the heart of the original Great White Way, right across Broadway from the new Metropolitan Opera House (1883). The Casino's interior was famous for its lavish decorations. With all walls painted in rich colors and studded with imitation jewels, and with its the boxes and interior fittings unashamedly ornate, the house was a true precursor of the 1920s' movie palaces. A ground-level cafe and New York's first roof garden were also part of the building. The Casino opened with *The Queen's Lace Handkerchief* (1882) by Johann Strauss (the Younger), the first of many similar musical productions, including a revival of Strauss's opera *Die Fledermaus* in 1885. After a long-simmering dispute between Aronson and his stockholders, he was ousted as manager in 1893. George Lederer

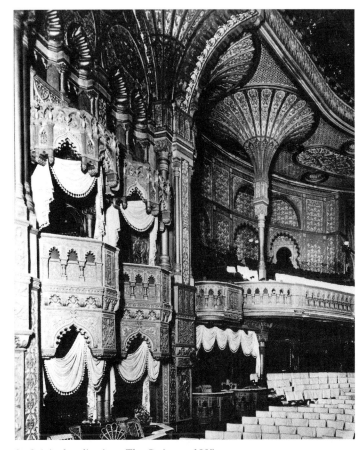

2 Original auditorium, The Casino, c. 1905

took over and produced several successes, most famously *Florodora* (1900), with its popular sextet of "pretty maidens." In 1902 the Shuberts leased the theatre and opened with a hit show imported from London, *A Chinese Honeymoon* . After a devastating fire in 1905, they rebuilt the Casino, moving the box office from 39th Street to Broadway, lowering the orchestra fifteen feet to take over the cafe space, and converting the former main floor into a balcony. This and other renovations over the years increased the seating capacity from the original 875 to 1458. The Casino reopened with another hit, a "merry English musical whirl" called *The Earl and the Girl* and starring Eddie Foy. The operetta formula remained popular through the 1920s—the Shuberts did well with old-fashioned shows like Rudolph Friml's *The Vagabond King* (1925) and Sigmund Romberg's *The Desert Song* (1926)— but the Casino's days were numbered. The theatre and its neighbor, the Knickerbocker Theatre (formerly Abbey's), were both demolished in 1930, replaced by loft-and-office towers.

1 From the outside the Casino looked like a showman's conception of an Arab emir's castle, complete with colonnaded balconies and towers. The fire escapes were unsightly but necessary—fire was an ever-present danger in gaslight New York.

2 Seating in the original auditorium was in the orchestra and single balcony and sixteen proscenium and loge boxes. Above the balcony a buffet floor provided tables where patrons could eat and drink while listening to the musical program. The stunning and colorful decor and the plush orchestra seats received rave reviews from critics and patrons alike.

Standard Theatre

1285-87 Broadway & 102 West 33rd Street

J. B. McElfatrick & Sons, Architects • Opened Dec. 23, 1884; 1100 seats • Reopened as Manhattan Theatre, Aug. 30,1887

A leading playhouse of the 1880s and '90s, the Standard was built on the site of the Eagle Variety Theatre (1875), which burned down in 1883. In its early years the theatre had a succession of managers who put on some notable productions, including Reginald DeKoven's *Robin Hood* (1891) and the U.S. premiere of Brandon Thomas's enduring *Charley's Aunt* (1893). The house was renamed the Manhattan Theatre in 1897, and its gaslights were replaced with electrical fixtures. The next year the theatre was leased to two of New York's leading young producers, William A. Brady and Florenz Ziegfeld Jr. They mounted several successful productions, including *Way Down East* (1898), a tearjerker that played 361 performances and then became a stock-company standard, before leasing the theatre to Harrison Grey Fiske and his wife Minnie Maddern in 1901. The curtain fell for the last time in 1909, when the theatre was demolished to make way for Gimbel's Department Store.

1 The exterior of the Standard Theatre, in the shadow of the Sixth Avenue El, was narrow and nondescript. Only the houseboards and a pair of sidewalk lanterns gave any indication of the showplace within.

2 The auditorium was narrow, with a maxiumum of 13 seats on each side of a center aisle, but with good-size first and second balconies. The proscenium boxes, made of plaster painted to simulate carved wood and draped in rich fabric, were the most prominent decorative feature.

2 Manhattan Theatre, interior, 1900

Broadway Theatre

1445 Broadway, 571-81 Seventh Avenue, & 158-68 West 41st Street

J. B. McElfatrick & Sons, Architects • Opened March 3, 1888; 1700 seats

The Broadway Theatre at 41st Street was the seventh playhouse in New York to bear that name (the first was opened in 1837, at Canal Street). The new theatre was a joint venture between the landowner, Count Elliott Zaborski, and producers T. Henry French and Frank Sanger. Their first hit was a dramatization of *Little Lord Fauntleroy* (1889), with actress Elsie Leslie in the title role. Other successes included Edwin Booth's final New York appearance, in *Hamlet* (1891), and Victor Herbert's first opera to be performed, *Prince Ananias* (1894). In 1899 another team of producers, Jacob Litt and Bart Dingwell, signed a ten-year lease for the Broadway and opened with William Young's dramatization of Lew Wallace's *Ben-Hur*. Klaw & Erlanger's spectacular production of this popular novel had a cast of hundreds and a simulated chariot race that was the talk of the city. The Shuberts added the Broadway to their growing portfolio of theatres in 1909, holding it until 1913, when Marcus Loew came in with silent movies. B. S. Moss leased the house in 1919, merging his circuit with Keith-Albee the following year. For most of the 1920s vaudeville and film presentations at popular prices proved to be

2 Artist's rendering of Broadway interior, toward house left

successful. Competitive pressures eventually made the Broadway redundant, however, and the building was demolished in 1929.

1   The Broadway's facade was undistinguished red brick and terra-cotta in a style that might best be termed Victorian commercial. Offices and other commercial tenants occupied most of this side of the property, with storefronts flanking the narrow center entrance that led patrons to an interior lobby and the auditorium.

2   The interior of the theatre was decorated in Moorish, or, as the press of the day called it, Persian style, echoing the much more finished appointments of the Casino. The hoods over the proscenium boxes were said to be of Persian derivation, as were the hanging antique copper chandeliers.

Garden Theatre

55-61 Madison Avenue & 22-32 East 27th Street

McKim, Mead & White, Architects • Opened September 27, 1890; 1200 seats

The Garden was the only theatre in New York designed by the eminent firm of McKim, Mead & White. It was part of the firm's Madison Square Garden, which was completed in 1890 and occupied a full square block (about two acres). The Garden Theatre was in the northwest corner of the building, with entrances at Madison Avenue and East 27th Street. Managed initially by Albert M. Palmer as a repertory house, the Garden was a success, attracting what today would be called upscale audiences for performers such as Sarah Bernhardt, Lillian Russell, and Richard Mansfield. Noteworthy presentations included the American premieres of Reginald DeKoven's *The Algerian* (1893) and Edmund Rostand's classic *Cyrano de Bergerac* (1898). Charles Frohman became manager in 1896

2   Garden Theatre box office lobby, 1925

and continued the Garden's high standard of bookings, but Manhattan's theatre district had begun to move uptown. After 1906, when architect Stanford White was murdered as he watched a performance on the Garden Roof, the Garden Theatre lost its luster. It soon became part of the so-called subway circuit, where successful Broadway productions had second runs in New York City neighborhood theatres. Frohman died in 1915, and the house became a venue for the Yiddish Art Theatre as well as for amateur groups and motion pictures. The entire Madison Square Garden complex was demolished in 1925 and replaced by a Romanesque skyscraper designed by the noted architect Cass Gilbert, as the headquarters of the New York Life Insurance Company.

3   Garden Theatre Auditorium, 1925

1   The ornate exterior of Madison Square Garden was faced with yellow brick and Pompeian terra-cotta and surrounded by a colonnaded arcade sheltering the sidewalks. On the roof was a tower, modeled on the Giralda (Seville) and surmounted by a statue of the goddess Diana by the American sculptor Augustus Saint-Gaudens.

2   Both the inner and outer lobbies of the Garden Theatre had mosaic tile floors and etched glass windows above the arches, which were lined with Ionic columns. Metal fittings and Italian marble facing added to the classical look of both lobbies. Lighting throughout was elegant and subdued.

3   Stanford White and his team of architects provided an elegant interior for the Garden Theatre. They introduced Beaux Arts classicism to playhouse design, inaugurating a new formalism and standard of decor that would influence theatre architects for the next four decades. The coffered sounding board, the swag and lattice box fronts, and the Corinthian columns flanking both boxes and proscenium are especially noteworthy.

Harrigan's Theatre

63-67 West 35th Street • Francis Hatch Kimball, Architect

Opened December 29, 1890; 910 seats • Reopened as Garrick Theatre, April 23, 1895

1

Edward Harrigan was a prominent theatrical personality, half of the entertainer-producer team of Harrigan and Hart. On his own in 1890, he built and named for himself a theatre just off Herald Square. For five years Harrigan's featured his work, opening with the play *Reilly and the 400.* When the actor Richard Mansfield took over the house in 1895, he saved half the letters on the signs and renamed the theatre for another actor, David Garrick. The name stayed but Mansfield departed, and impresario Charles Frohman became manager. He staged a virtually unbroken string of hits until his death aboard the *Lusitania* in 1915. William Gillette, George Bernard Shaw, David Belasco, and George M. Cohan were just a few of the names associated with Frohman's years at the Garrick. The Shuberts bought the house in 1916 and leased it to financier Otto Kahn, who renamed it

2   Contemporary drawing of the auditorium, Harrigan's Theatre, 1890

for the Theatre du Vieux Columbier, a French company led by the avant-garde actor/director Jacques Copeau. Kahn had designer Raymond Antonin and architect Herbert Krapp create a small, single-balcony theatre seating 541. The French productions were artistic successes but financial failures, and Kahn was persuaded to offer the house to the newly organized Theatre Guild. Beginning in 1919, the Guild staged a number of distinguished dramas,

including G. B. Shaw's *Heartbreak House* (1920) and *Saint Joan* (1923) at the renamed Garrick. The Guild moved to new headquarters on West 52nd Street in 1925, and the Garrick reverted to Shubert management. The next four years were enlived by two productions of Rodgers and Hart's *Garrick Gaieties* (1925; 1926) and two Eugene O'Neill plays from the Provincetown Players. In 1929 the Garrick became a burlesque house, and in 1932 it was razed.

1   The Garrick Theatre's buff brick exterior was heavily ornamented with the terra-cotta detailing that architect Kimball had introduced to New York theatre construction. The arrangement of the facade into three central arched window openings flanked by side bays was based on European prototypes and would become a standard treatment for theatre exteriors in the United States for decades to come.

2   The auditorium at Harrigan's was an opulently styled melange of ornamental plaster, canopied boxes, domed ceiling, and backlit stained glass. The ecclesisastical feeling conveyed by this drawing came easily to Kimball, who had designed many churches in the New York area.

Empire Theatre

1426-28 Broadway & 116-22 West 40th Street

J. B. McElfatrick & Co., Architects • Opened January 25, 1893; 1099 Seats

For six decades the Empire was considered by many on Broadway to be the top theatre in New York. It was built by Frank Sanger and Al Hayman for producer Charles Frohman, who opened with a David Belasco play that became a hit, *The Girl I Left Behind Me*. Many productions came to the Empire from Europe. Frohman had particular success with the work of British playwright J. M. Barrie, especially *Peter Pan* (1905). Despite its early success, the Empire was never considered an architecturally attractive house. Thus, when Frohman's lease came up for renewal, he asked for and got a top-to-bottom alteration. The McElfatricks' original work on the Empire consisted of a narrow Broadway entrance leading to a typically well-planned auditorium decorated in a hodgepodge of styles, fronting on 40th Street. In 1903 Carrere & Hastings (architects of the New York Public Library on 42nd Street and other landmarks) created a formal procession of interior spaces, each more richly detailed than its predecessor. After Frohman's death in 1915, management of the Empire was taken over by Al Hayman, who brought in Paramount-Famous Players. They had some successes, most notably with Katharine Cornell in *The Barretts of Wimpole Street* (1931). Paramount then withdrew, but the Haymans carried on, striking box office gold with Lindsay & Crouse's *Life with Father* (1939–45). The comedy still holds the record as longest-running non-musical Broadway play. Other successes followed, including Carson McCullers' dramatization of her novel *The* *Member of the Wedding* (1950). Eventually, commercial pressures forced the demolition of the old theatre, which gave way to an office building in 1953.

2   Auditorium, Empire Theatre, 1893

1   The marquee and main entrance of the Empire were on Broadway in a handsome, if narrow, office tower, built in the conventional New York style of the time. The lobbies beyond the entrance led to the large auditorium, located around the corner on West 40th Street, where the price of real estate was less expensive.

2   The original workmanlike, Victorian interior of the Empire, decorated in details taken from disparate sources and periods, was much admired in its day, but the view-stealing columns and stiff chairs were outmoded virtually from the first day.

3 In 1903, the firm of Carrere & Hastings redecorated the Empire in a more luxurious Louis XIV style. In this photo, taken forty-four years later, the theatre still has the glow of a successful, prosperous enterprise.

4 The Empire had large, elegant lobbies. The entrance vestibule, lined in Caen stone, led to the outer lobby, which was Georgian in inspiration and was lined with cream-colored walls divided into panels by paired Ionic pilasters. Both outer and inner lobbies were decorated with portraits of great actors and actresses who had played at the Empire. This gallery was augmented over the years, and included paintings of Katharine Cornell, Otis Skinner, and Ethel Barrymore.

4 Inner lobby, Empire Theatre, 1947

American Theatre

260-62 West 42nd Street, 644-48 Eighth Avenue, & 245-59 West 41st Street

Charles Coolidge Haight, Architect • Opened May 22, 1893; 2064 seats

◄ 1

2 Drawing of American Theatre exterior, from 41st Street, ca. 1893

The site theatrical manager T. Henry French chose for his new entertainment center over a century ago was derided as being too far away from the established theatre district. Nevertheless, he went ahead and built the American Theatre in the blockfront on Eighth Avenue between 42nd and 41st streets. His 42nd Street entrance was small, in keeping with the neighboring brownstones, but inside the walls was the fourth-largest auditorium in the city, and atop the structure was an open-air roof garden. The theatre opened with one of French's spectacular productions, *The Prodigal Daughter*. The show was a hit, but after it ended a profitable run, the American began its long decline. French was indeed ahead of his time, and besides, the American was not an especially attractive venue. The auditorium was dotted with view-obstructing columns used to support the balcony, and people in the standing room galleries above the second balcony could only hear but not see the show on stage. French's interests were foreclosed in 1897—his father, theatrical publisher Samuel French, was among the creditors—and the American came under the management of Henry Savage, who turned the stage over to repertory companies. He did only moderately well, as did several successors, and in 1908 William Morris brought top-line vaudeville acts to the renamed American Music Hall. He believed that the new American could succeed, and engaged architect Thomas Lamb to rebuild the roof garden as an enclosed theatre seating 1400. Lamb created a woodland arbor, with support pillars disguised as trees and twinkling electric lights to suggest stars in a nighttime sky. The theatregoing public failed to respond, however, and in 1911 Morris sold his interests to Marcus Loew's

3 Full house, American Theatre, 1906

1 The 42nd Street entrance to the American Theatre was comparatively modest, fitting in with the neighboring brownstone residences. The facade here, like the much grander front on 41st Street, was of buff brick trimmed with tan terra-cotta. *(Photo on previous page.)*

2 The 41st Street facade was large and had a ponderous quality more suited to an armory than a place of entertainment. The lines reminded some critics of the recently completed Carnegie Hall on Seventh Avenue and 57th Street.

3 With the fourth largest auditorium in the New York, the American often hosted special events. Here the house is packed for Ted Marks' Sixth Annual St. Patrick's Concert. The theatre was spacious and airy, with good sight lines except for more than a dozen view-blocking posts. On the ceiling a shallow central dome rested on pendentives.

organization. Under the name Loew's American Theatre, both the theatre's auditoriums were converted to a film-and-small-time-variety format. After a fire in 1930, the American was demolished. The Depression, the War, and the economic decline of the West 42nd Street neighborhood discouraged or deterred builders from making a major investment in the site, and the parking lot there remains in operation in 1999—almost seventy years, longer than the American's tenure of about forty years.

4   Original roof garden, American Theatre, c. 1900

5   Auditorium and proscenium, American Theatre, toward boxes and stage, c. 1900

4   The original roof garden at the American Theatre was bright and airy, but open to the elements. With a brick tile floor and the bandstand and service area on one side, the cafe was lighted by bare bulbs in arc pipes and conduits decorated to resemble palm trees. In the 1908 renovation an enclosed theatre seating 1400 and with rustic terraces as lounge areas replaced the garden.

5   The decor of the original American auditorium leaned toward the Classical—plaster swags and laurel wreaths on the box and balcony fronts, Ionic pillars and pilasters, and coffered ceiling arches. The curtain's ASBESTOS label was meant to reassure audiences that it was fireproof.

Abbey's Theatre

1394-1402 Broadway & 117-25 West 38th Street

J. B. McElfatrick & Co., Architects • Opened November 8, 1893 • Reopened as Knickerbocker Theatre, September 14, 1896

Built by Robert Goelet, a prominent New York landowner, Abbey's Theatre was named for impresario Henry Abbey, its first manager. Abbey died in 1896 and was replaced by Al Hayman of the Theatrical Syndicate, who gave the house a new name, Knickerbocker. Abbey's policy of booking mostly repertory companies, especially those led by Ellen Terry and Sir Henry Irving, was altered to bring in more musical comedies and operettas. Hayman booked Victor Herbert's longest-running hit, *Red Mill* (1906), which he advertised with Broadway's first moving electric sign. Hayman also presented dramas, including Maude Adams' debut in J. M. Barrie's *Quality Street* (1901). Klaw & Erlanger were the primary managers after 1911. Among their successful dramas were *Bulldog Drummond* (1921) and a revival of Barrie's *Peter Pan* (1924), but musicals dominated the Knickerbocker bill in the 1920s. Highlights included works by Vincent Youmans (*Lollipop*, 1924) and the new team of Rodgers and Hart (*Dearest Enemy*, 1925; *Honeymoon Lane*, 1926). The Knickerbocker and its neighbor to the north, the Casino, were both razed in 1930.

1 From the outside the Abbey looked more like an office building than a theatre. The entrance was on Broadway, given prominence by its arched opening flanked by a pair of columns and topped by an electric sign.

2 The Abbey had one of the grandest entrance halls on Broadway. The double-height, vaulted box office lobby had a mosaic tile floor, marble and onyx wainscotting, mahogany and leaded-glass doors, and a magnificent fireplace.

2 Lobby, Abbey's Theatre, 1893

Herald Square Theatre

1331 Broadway & 111-29 West 35th Street

Rose & Stone, Architects • Opened September 17, 1894; 1148 seats

◀ 1

In 1883, on the corner of Broadway and 35th Street, the New Park Theatre was erected on a site that had held a cyclorama, a dime museum, and the New York Aquarium. Actor/manager Charles Evans leased the house, rebuilt it, and named it the Herald Square Theatre. He opened with the American premiere of G. B. Shaw's *Arms and the Man* and followed with the David Belasco's first success as a playwright, *The Heart of Maryland* (1895). The Herald Square was also important to the Shubert brothers as the first New York house they leased (in 1900). Their first hit was *Dolly Varden* (1902). In 1908, while under sublease to comedian Lew Fields, the Broadway frontage of the Herald Square was destroyed by fire. Within months it was rebuilt as a one-story structure by Architect Charles Meyers. Fields reopened with a Victor Herbert operetta, *Old Dutch* (1909), in which nine-year-old Helen Hayes made her Broadway debut. Another first came in 1911, as the Herald Square became the first New York theatre to convert to showing silent films, under the management of Marcus Loew. In 1915, with the theatre district firmly established seven blocks to the north, the old theatre was replaced by an office building.

2   Part of proscenium arch, decorative curtain, Herald Square Theatre, 1897

1   The buff brick exterior of the the Herald Square Theatre was distinguished by a one-story colonnade of red marble. Portions of the New Park Theatre's outer walls were retained on the eastern end of the 35th Street facade. On Broadway, the frontage was given over to shops and to the corner box office.

2   The interior of the Herald Square was plain, especially when compared to some of its ornate neighbors. Decorative plasterwork was confined to the proscenium and box area. In keeping with the custom of the day, the curtain was decorated with a scene appropriate to the current production.

Hammerstein's Olympia

1514-26 Broadway, 163-69 West 44th Street, 162-70 West 45th Street • J. B. McElfatrick & Son, Architects

LYRIC THEATRE: Opened November 25, 1895; 1850 seats • OLYMPIA MUSIC HALL: Opened December 17, 1895; 3815 seats

Oscar Hammerstein's "colossal amusement enterprise," the Olympia, was the first major theatre to be built on Long Acre (soon-to-be-renamed Times) Square. Occupying the full block between 44th and 45th streets, the four-story showplace had three major performance spaces—the Music Hall, the Lyric Theatre, and a rooftop, glass-enclosed theatre/cafe—along with a small concert hall, rathskeller, billiard parlor, bowling alley, and Turkish bath. A single ticket gained a patron admission to all these attractions. Opening night was a mob scene, as crowds came more to see what Oscar had built than the acts he had booked. The Music Hall was spectacular, more European opera house than Broadway theatre, and included no less than 124 boxes and five balconies. The stage was opera-size, larger than what was necessary for the acrobats, jugglers, and comedians who soon dominated the entertainment. The Lyric was about half the size of the Music Hall but shared many of the same characteristics—84 boxes, four balconies, and pastry-chef plasterwork. Unfortunately, Oscar's grandiose vision was not matched by box office receipts. The two playhouses had to be rebuilt to

2   Auditorium, Olympia Music Hall, 1895

1   The Olympia's facade, clad in Indiana limestone and buff brick, was a jumble of Romanesque, French Renaissance, and vaguely Moorish elements, complicated by four different cornice lines and a dozen different window styles. Originally, the center entrance, emblazoned Hammerstein's Olympia, provided access to the entire complex. This photo reflects the 1898–99 renovation, when the main entrance led to the New York Theatre, and the Criterion entrance was on the corner of West 44th Street.

2   Decorated in what the contemporary press termed Louis XIV style, the original Olympia Music Hall was Oscar Hammerstein's fantasy of old Vienna come to life. Particularly noteworthy was the ornate creation above the proscenium, which depicted the goddess Fame crowning two figures representing Poetry and Prose. Oscar had built an opera-size stage and a huge, opulent house for the carriage trade that seldom came to see his variety shows. Lit by a glorious chandelier, the space survived in this form a short seven years.

3 Lyric Theatre, 1895

more conventional designs in 1897, when the boxes and all but two balconies were eliminated. Still, the lenders foreclosed in 1898 and leased the Lyric to producer Charles Frohman, who renamed it the Criterion and began a successful run that lasted almost seventeen years. Among his hit shows was Clyde Fitch's *Barbara Frietchie* (1900). The Music Hall also survived Hammerstein's collapse. After an interim management, Klaw & Erlanger bought the entire Olympia complex and rebuilt the big hall as a conventional theatre with 1675 seats and a new name, New York. Among their notable presentations were four George M. Cohan musicals—including *Forty-five Minutes from Broadway* (1906)—Victor Herbert's operetta *Naughty Marietta* (1910), and the *Ziegfeld Follies of 1912*. William Morris became manager in 1913, but movie magnate Marcus Loew took over the William Morris organization in 1915. In that same year Charles Frohman died and his theatre became a movie house. Loew also converted Morris's theatre into a prime Times Square film/vaudeville showcase. During the 1920s, as Loew's State and other movie palaces were opened, the old Olympia complex began to decline. The entire building was finally demolished in 1935, replaced by a nightclub and dancehall called the International Casino (architects: Thomas Lamb and Eugene DeRosa) and a movie theatre, the new Criterion, which remained in operation through the 1990s. In 1988 the club space was divided into a number of small spaces, which were leased to the off-Broadway Roundabout Theatre Company in 1991.

3 The Lyric Theatre auditorium was decorated in the Louis XVI style. It had much the same look as the neighboring Music Hall, but on a smaller scale. It seemed that every available space was covered with some kind of decoration. On the ceiling was a European-style mural depicting classical figures. The chandelier there was striking, but less ornate than the one in the Music Hall. Caryatids supported the second tier of boxes.

Hammerstein's Victoria

1473-81 Broadway & 201-205 West 42nd Street

J. B. McElfatrick & Son, Architects • Opened March 2, 1899; 950 seats

In 1898 a penniless but irrepressibly optimistic Oscar Hammerstein managed to lease a site at the corner of Seventh Avenue and 42nd Street occupied by a livery stable and former carbarn. Here, with money begged and borrowed, he built his new theatre, using the demolition debris as filler for the exterior walls and buying used but still elegant furnishings and carpeting for the interior. In March 1899 the Victoria opened, the new name chosen, Oscar told the press, "because I have been victorious over mine enemies," his creditors. A month later, he transferred ownership of the Victoria to his sons and declared personal bankruptcy. Under Hammerstein family management the theatre had modest success, with eleven legitimate productions featuring stars like Marie Dressler and the Rogers Brothers in its first four years. The Venetian Terrace Roof Garden, opened on June 26, 1901, and remodeled as the Paradise Roof Garden in 1901, was an unqualified success. Downstairs, the Hammersteins enjoyed another triumph when the Victoria became a "theatre of varieties." The marquee now advertised Barnumesque attractions—freak acts, novelties, and celebrities such as the boxers Jim Corbett and Jack Johnson. The Victoria then became the now-booming Times Square's premier vaudeville house, booking big-time acts such as Bert Williams, W.C. Fields, and the four Cohans. The ensuing box office bonanza filled the Hammerstein coffers once again. Oscar turned his attention to his long-dreamt-of Manhattan Opera House, a project that consumed the Victoria's profits and then some. Despite the best efforts of Oscar's able sons, Willie and Arthur, the aging impresario was forced to sell his Times Square vaudeville franchise to E.F. Albee in 1913. More interested in getting rid of a competitor than in developing the Victoria, Albee deserted the theatre after his new Palace opened in 1915. The building was condemned and demolished, replaced by the Rialto, a movie house designed by Thomas Lamb.

1   One of the most familiar photographs of the "Crossroads of the World," taken in 1908, centers on Hammerstein's entertainment complex on the northwest corner. Just west of the Victoria is another playhouse built by Oscar, the old Theatre Republic (renamed the Belasco, 1902–1910, and restored as the New Victory in 1997).
(Photo on previous page.)

2   From the outset Oscar Hammerstein had planned for a roof garden atop the Victoria. At first there was merely an open-air terrace cafe, but soon a shed roof and stage were added. In 1900 the café tables were replaced by 600 theatre seats, and the newly named Paradise Roof Garden became a favorite place for New Yorkers and tourists alike. With its something-for-everyone approach to entertainment, flamboyant promotions, and raffish show-business glamor, the roof garden established the character of 42nd Street for decades to come.

2   Paradise Roof Garden, 1908

Theatre Republic

207-11 West 42nd Street • Albert E. Westover, Architect

Opened September 27, 1900; 982 seats • Reopened as Belasco Theatre, September 29, 1902

Oscar Hammerstein built his third Long Acre Square playhouse, the Theatre Republic, based on his desire to expand the successful Paradise Roof Garden atop Hammerstein's Victoria right next door. The Republic itself was comparatively small, suited only for drama and thus of little interest to the flamboy- ant Oscar. He abdicated after two seasons and leased the house to David Belasco, who was then establish- ing himself as an independent producer. Belasco quickly renamed the theatre for himself and invested several hundred thousand dollars in a major remod- eling. His architects, Bigelow, Wallis & Cotten, gutted the original interior—a Victorian confection replete with plump cherubs, Viennese pastry plasterwork, and a large ceiling dome covered in gold leaf—and installed a low- key auditorium decorated in subdued tones of brown and green. The major decorative features were murals of pas- toral settings by Rudolph Allen on the orchestra walls. Technologically, Belasco's house was state-of-the-art: lighting was raised and dimmed by rheostats, their first use in a Broadway theatre, and complex machinery (for

2   Original auditorium, Theatre Republic, 1900

1   The exterior of Hammerstein's smallish Theatre Republic was nevertheless an imposing brick and brownstone addition to the burgeoning theatre row on 42nd Street in 1900. David Belasco's elegant iron-and- glass marquee was added in 1902. Both marquee and exte- rior staircase were removed in 1910, when the city widened the roadway on 42nd Street. The stairway was restored in the 1995 renovation.
    (Photo on previous page.)

2   The original auditorium owed more to 19th-century Middle Europe than to 20th-century America. Its plump cherubs, Viennese plasterwork, and large ceiling dome covered in gold leaf did not make up for the cramped stage with mini- mal wing space, the lack of dressing room space, and poor sight lines from the side bal- conies.

Belasco's famous stage effects) was installed beneath the stage. What Belasco did not fix was the cramped stage with minimal wing space, the poor sight lines from many balcony seats, and the tiny box office lobby, which was tucked under the outside stairway. Nevertheless, the theatre prospered as a showcase for Belasco's own plays, including *The Warrens of Virginia* (1907) starring Cecil B. DeMille and Mary Pickford. After Belasco became involved with the newer, larger Stuyvesant (1907; renamed Belasco 1910), Hammerstein ended his lease and brought in A. H. Woods, "the melodrama king." Woods renamed the theatre Republic and produced revivals of *Lilac Time* (1917) and other old favorites. His major success

came when he booked *Abie's Irish Rose* (1921), an ethnic comedy that had been panned by the critics when it opened at the Fulton (Folies Bergeres) Theatre. *Abie* caught the public's fancy and ran for a record-breaking 2,327 performances. Along with other 42nd Street theatres, the Republic lost its theatrical lustre in the late 1920s. It became part of Minsky's chain of burlesque theatres (1930) before being converted into a grind film house (1942) with a new wartime name, Victory. The theatre kept the name but not the spirit until the 1990s. Then, as part of the ambitious Times Square Redevelopment Project, the theatre was restored to its Belasco glory and reopened as the New Victory.

3 Hammerstein's old theatre on 42nd Street was restored to its Belasco-era elegance as a part of New York's 1990s renewal program for the Times Square theatre district. The comprehensive renovation cost over $11 million, and the theatre was opened to the public in 1995 as the city's first legitimate theatre for children and families, the New Victory.

➤ **3** Restored auditorium, New Victory Theatre, 1997

Schley Music Hall

112 West 34th Street & 109-11 West 33rd Street • Michael Bernstein, Architect

Opened February 26, 1900; 841 seats • Reopened as Savoy Theatre, October 8, 1900

In one of the fastest name changes in theatrical history, this small music hall became the Savoy Theatre less than eight months after its grand opening. The Schley also changed managers in its early years. Charles Kraus, Alfred Aarons, and Hyde & Behrman all came and went before the Savoy was leased to the renowned producer Charles Frohman, who made it the sixth successful house he controlled in New York. Among his early hits were two dramatizations of popular novels, *Soldier of Fortune* (1902) and *Mrs. Wiggs of the Cabbage Patch* (1904), and George Broadhurst's long-running drama of political corruption, *The Man of the Hour* (1906). Plays by William Butler Yeats and Lady Gregory, performed by the Irish Players of Dublin, were also booked into the Savoy. After Frohman's interest turned uptown and he declined to renew his lease, the Savoy was converted to a motion picture theatre. It continued operating until 1952, when it was demolished, the last remnant of Herald Square's brief moment in the history of the Broadway theatre.

2 Auditorium and proscenium, Savoy Theatre, 1900

1 The Schley Music Hall, financed by Tammany Hall politican "Big Tim" Sullivan, was built within the walls of three town houses. The two on West 33rd Street held the stage and auditorium, while a 15-footer on West 34th Street housed the narrow but well-designed entrance. A two-story terra-cotta portico and a decorative marquee disguised the theatre's domestic origins.

2 Crowded onto a 50-by-100-foot lot, the two-balcony Schley auditorium was long and slender, with a high ceiling. Stylistically, the interior was typical of its architect's work—heavy, late-Victorian plasterwork around the proscenium and boxes, with plain side walls and post-supported balconies. The seats could be folded in pairs to facilitate cleaning.

Majestic Theatre

5 Columbus Circle & 309-13 West 58th Street • John H. Duncan, Architect

Opened January 21, 1903; 1704 seats • Reopened as Park Theatre, October 23, 1911

When the tiny Pabst Hotel on Broadway and 42nd Street was demolished to make way for the Times Tower in 1902, the Pabst Brewing Company decided to move uptown. In partnership with investors Andrew Flake and Robert Dowling the Pabsts erected a new café, theatre, and roof garden on The Grand Circle (soon to be renamed Columbus Circle). The Majestic was the first theatre by John Duncan, best known for his design of Grant's Tomb. Edward Stair and A.L. Wilbur, the theatre's first managers, opened with two of the top shows of 1903—the first musical version of *The Wizard of Oz* and Victor Herbert's hit *Babes in Toyland*—but then had a run of mediocre bookings until they were replaced in 1911 by two partners in the Theatrical Syndicate, Frank McGee and William Harris. The location of the Majestic—ten blocks north of the Times Square theatre district—made it difficult to attract top shows, but the partners had some success not only with musicals but also with dramas; G. B. Shaw's *Pygmalion*, starring Mrs. Patrick Campbell, had its American premiere at the theatre in 1914.

A group of investors headed by William Randolph Hearst bought the building in 1914. They did not institute major changes until 1923, when the renovated theatre reopened as the Cosmopolitan, the New York showcase for Hearst's Cosmopolitan Pictures. After *Little Old New York* and several other silent films, Hearst changed course and leased the theatre to a succession of managers, including Flo Ziegfeld, Earl Carroll, the Shuberts, and the composer Vincent Youmans. The house (or its location) failed to attract audiences—even Youmans's beautifully scored *Great Day!* was a disappointment—but the theatre made it through the 1930s and '40s with a mix of second-run films and low-priced vaudeville. Legitimate theatre returned to Columbus Circle in 1944 with the Theatre Guild's *Sing Out, Sweet Land,* followed the

2   Auditorium, toward house right, Majestic Theatre, 1903

next year by Maurice Evans in *G.I. Hamlet.* Over the years the theatre continued to acquire new names: *Theatre for Young People* (1934), *Park* (cinema; 1935), *International* (1944; 1946), and *Columbus Circle* (1945). The old Majestic ended its days as one of the first television theatres. It was used by NBC from 1949 until 1954, when it was razed as part of the New York Coliseum convention center development.

1   The facade of the brand-new Majestic Theatre was dominated by the Pabst Grand Circle Café, at left. The small theatre entrance was marked by a six-story domed tower topped by a small, light-studded globe. The brick and stone building was in a style sometimes referred to as Edwardian Baroque.

2   Among the innovative features of the Majestic was the use of cantilevered steel beams to hang the balconies over the orchestra without the support of stage-blocking columns. The auditorium was decorated in tones of ivory, green, and gold, with richly ornamented plasterwork in the Beaux Arts style. Watered silk panels covered the walls.

Lyric Theatre

213 West 42nd Street & 214-26 West 43rd Street

Victor Hugo Koehler, Architect • Opened October 12, 1903; 1350 seats

The Lyric was originally built by developer Eugene C. Potter as a home for composer Reginald DeKoven's American School of Opera. The school went bankrupt before construction was finished, however, and Potter leased the theatre and its offices to the Shubert brothers. Among their bookings were *The Chocolate Soldier* (1909), an operetta by Oscar Straus based on Shaw's *Arms and the Man*, and three operettas by Rudolph Friml—*The Firefly* (1912), *High Jinx* (1913), and *Katinka* (1916). After World War I motion pictures began alternating with live entertainment such as *For Goodness Sake* (1922), with Fred and Adele Astaire. The Oppenheimer brothers took over the management in 1925. That same year the Lyric came alive with the Irving Berlin-

2 Lyric Theatre, 42nd Street facade, 1903

George S. Kaufman-Marx Brothers hit *Cocoanuts* (1925), which was made into one of the first talking pictures in 1929. Cole Porter's first hit, *Fifty Million Frenchmen* (1929), was the Lyric's last. The theatre soon became part of the "new" 42nd Street, switching to an all-film bill in 1934. In the ensuing years the boxes and most of the original decor were removed. By the 1980s the Lyric was in as bad a shape as the rest of the 42nd Street theatres. But then, in 1996, the property was leased by Livent, a Canadian corporation, which converted the Lyric and the adjoining Apollo Theatre into the Ford Center for the Performing Arts. (There is additional text coverage of this spectacular renovation on the pages devoted to the Times Square /Apollo.)

1 The Lyric was one of only a few New York theatres that had two formal entrances. The façade on 43rd Street was wide and had a design reminiscent of the Opera Comique in Paris. Of the five entryways, those under the stylish iron-and-glass marquee led to a small vestibule off the orchestra; those to the left and right both led to the gallery and balcony. The elaborately carved windows and other elegant features look much the same today as in this century-old photograph. Just below the cornice is a large rehearsal hall where many of the early Shubert shows took shape.

2 A narrow, ornate entrance amid the brownstones of 42nd Street (where frontage was expensive) opened onto a long corridor that led to a separate building on 43rd Street. There the auditorium was built on an east-west axis, allowing for greater seating capacity and stage room than in most conventional north-south plans.

3 Victor Hugo Koehler's designs for the Lyric Theatre were not completely successful. The posts supporting the balconies obstructed the view from many seats, and some critics found the skull-cap dome on the ceiling to be gratuitous. The profuse decoration around the boxes was balanced by the flatness of the rest of the house. The eighteen boxes—nine to each side— were far too many for a commercial theatre of this size, and many were removed soon after the Lyric opened.

◀ 3 Lyric auditorium, 1903

Hudson Theatre

139-41 West 44th Street & 136-44 West 45th Street

J. B. McElfatrick & Son and Israels & Harder, Architects • Opened October 19, 1903; 1048 seats

The almost 100-year-old Hudson Theatre has survived most of its contemporaries despite its location, unfashionably east of Times Square. It was built by Henry B. Harris, scion of a family of theatre operators and one of the Theatrical Syndicate's leading young producers. The McElfatrick firm began the job and Israels and Harder finished it, but at what point and for what reason are both unknown. Behind the theatre's unremarkable facade was a delightfully ornate interior. The building was designed as Harris's showcase and headquarters, and he allowed a generous budget for construction. The new playhouse opened with Ethel Barrymore in *Cousin Kate* (1903), followed by Shaw's *Man and Superman* (1905) and other distinguished plays. After Harris's untimely death aboard the *Titanic* in 1912, his wife René, who survived the disaster,

2   Auditorium, Hudson Theatre, 1903

took over the Hudson. She did well with a variety of bookings, from popular but unmemorable George M. Cohan productions to more serious fare such as Sean O'Casey's *The Plough and the Stars* (1927). Like most New York theatre owners, René Harris was devastated by the Depression. Unable to meet expenses, she lost the Hudson to foreclosure. In 1934, the theatre was leased to CBS for use as a radio studio. But three years later the Hudson rebounded as a legitimate house and in 1939 came under Shubert management. *Arsenic & Old Lace* (1941) transferred from the Fulton Theatre and finished its long run at the Hudson. The team of Howard Lindsay and Russel Crouse, flush with cash from their phenomenal hit *Life With Father*, bought the Hudson in 1944 and the next year opened their Pulitzer Prize-winning play *State of the Union* there. Another hit

was Sidney Kingsley's *Detective Story* (1949). NBC bought the theatre in 1950 and converted it into a television studio for *Broadway Open House* (1950–54) and *The Tonight Show* (1954–59). Stage presentations then came back, most notably Lillian Hellman's *Toys in the Attic* (1960) and Ann Corio's *This Was Burlesque* (1965). After 1968 the old playhouse went through several changes of ownership and entertainment format porno films (renamed the Avon-Hudson, 1968), rock concerts, and disco dancing (renamed the Savoy, 1981). The Hudson was designated a landmark building in 1987, making it impossible for a developer to raze the theatre without proving economic hardship. Faced with these restrictions, the owners of the adjacent Hotel Macklowe rescinded their plans to demolish the Hudson and, instead, converted it into a conference center.

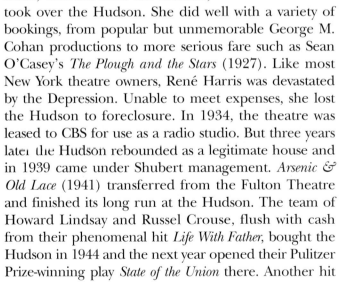

1   The gray brick and limestone facade of the Hudson Theatre was domestic in both scale and character; it fit in well with neighboring brownstone residences. The modest-size marquee quietly announced the theatre's name and its current star, the great actor Henry Miller. Manager Sam Harris's offices were above the entrance. Medusa-head capitals decorate the pilasters in the center of the architectural composition.

2   Wood paneling lines the walls of both the orchestra and first balcony, and the proscenium boxes are flanked by columns of the composite order. Above the arch the sounding board is comprised of hexagonal coffers rimmed by a row of light bulbs. Bulbs are also set in geometric constellations in the ceiling, creating a magical effect. One novel feature, no longer extant, is the varicolored Favrille glass patternwork lining the box and balcony fronts and the inner proscenium arch.

New Amsterdam Theatre

214 West 42nd Street & 207-19 West 41st Street

Herts & Tallant, Architects • Opened October 26, 1903; 1702 Seats

Flagship of the Klaw & Erlanger empire, the New Amsterdam for many years was regarded as the crown jewel of 42nd Street, before it became a tawdry second-run movie house in the 1940s. A rare example of the Art Nouveau style—which its architects knew well from their student days in Paris—the New Amsterdam was the embodiment of the Beaux Arts ideal of cogent planning wedded to a design in which both painting and sculpture are full and equal partners with architecture. The sparkling new theatre opened with a production of Shakespeare's *Midsummer Night's Dream*, followed by a series of musical shows and visiting repertory productions. Among the outstanding shows were George M. Cohan's *Forty-five Minutes from Broadway* (1906), Franz Lehar's *The Merry Widow* (1907), and Victor Herbert's *Sweethearts* (1913). As the principal home of the *Ziegfeld Follies* from 1913 until 1927, the New Amsterdam achieved a theatrical aura commensurate with its outstanding architecture, allowing the house to flourish long after its neighbors had become movie houses. After Ziegfeld, the 1930 edition of *The Earl Carroll Vanities* played to

2 Auditorium, house left, New Amsterdam Theatre, 1903

packed houses, along with Irving Berlin's *Face the Music* (1932). The New Amsterdam theatre complex had a unique arrangement, consisting of a narrow, ten-story office building on 42nd Street with auditorium and stage house in a separate structure on 41st Street. The two buildings were linked by a hyphenlike one-story chamber at ground level and a bridge seven stories above the ground that gave access to the roof garden. The Aerial Gardens opened on June 6, 1904, with 693 seats. It had a full proscenium and stage house in addition to an open-air terrace. Initially meant for summer use, the roof garden was enclosed by large windows that were intended to be opened in pleasant weather. In 1915 the roof was redesigned by designer Joseph Urban to feature a dance floor and ramps for the chorus girls around a U-shaped balcony, and reopening as the Ziegfeld Danse de Follies. Ziegfeld put on a series of midnight revues called the *Frolics* and headlined by some of the same stars appearing in the main theatre downstairs. The onset of Prohibition sent most patrons off to basement speakeasies, and

1 The original entrance to the New Amsterdam was a narrow, elegant Art Nouveau masterpiece echoing its architects' training at the famed École des Beaux Arts in Paris. The limestone and terra-cotta facade consisted of a three-story arched entryway enlivened by paired columns and surmounted by a grouping of five statues—a knight and a maid flanking classical representations of Music, Drama, and Comedy. Atop the theatre were seven stories of offices and, on the roof, the Aerial Gardens.

2 The theatre's auditorium was on West 41st Street, entered via a one-story connecting foyer. The interior design was one of New York City's finest examples of the Art Deco style. Vines and flowers were among the primary motifs. Allegorical murals by Blum and Wenzell filled the walls above the proscenium and boxes with fanciful representations of Drama, Poetry, Music, Morality, Truth, and Romance. Rich wainscotting lined the side walls.

3 Lobby entrance, New Amsterdam Theatre, 1903

Ziegfeld moved on to more suitable venues. As for the New Amsterdam, after a series of stints as a radio studio, television theatre, and rehearsal spaces, it was gutted as part of the effort to return the main auditorium to legitimate use. The project was stalled first by the discovery of structural weaknesses in the building brought on by years of neglect and then by political and financial problems that stalled the much-touted renewal of 42nd Street. In 1994 the Walt Disney Company began a program to renovate the New Amsterdam as a home for its own productions. After a multimillion-dollar renovation planned by architect Hugh Hardy, the New Amsterdam reopened with Disney's *The Lion King* in 1997.

3 Over the lobby entrance to the New Amsterdam was Hugh Tallant's allegorical interpretation of "Progress." On one side of the lobby were Hinton Perry's recreations of the Dutch colony of New Amsterdam, on the other side, the New York skyline of 1903.

4 The stage was the largest ever designed for a legitimate theatre. It was sectioned into a series of elevator platforms and had a revolving turntable which allowed for spectacular scenic effects.

4 Auditorium toward proscenium, New Amsterdam Theatre, 1903

5 Both balconies were cantilevered, the upper one supported additionally by thin guy wires anchored in the mammoth beams that supported the roof garden.

6 At the rear of the auditorium a vaulted promenade ran from side to side, with stairs at either end to the balcony and down to a large ovate space, the Amsterdam Room. Here murals by James Wall Finn commemorated significant moments in the history of New York City, including the arrival from Holland of Governor Peter Stuyvesant, the founding of the New York Stock Exchange, and the first voyage of Robert Fulton's steamboat *Clermont.*

5   Auditorium toward balcony, New Amsterdam Theatre, 1903

6   Lounge, New Amsterdam Theatre, 1903

Lyceum Theatre

149-57 West 45th Street & 152 West 46th Street

Herts & Tallant, Architects • Opened November 2, 1903; 952 seats

The Lyceum is the oldest continuously operating legitmate theatre in New York and the first to be designated a city landmark (1974). Built of gray limestone, and with a penthouse apartment and rehearsal hall tucked under its mansard roof, the theatre also had a seven-story extension behind the stage that held studios for scenery and costume designers and craftsworkers. (The apartment and studios are now the site of the Shubert Archives, one of the world's most comprehensive research collections.) Producer Daniel Frohman conceived the Lyceum as a major improvement on his 14th Street theatre of the same name. When the theatre opened, it was a model stock company house, but it soon became a "combination house," leased to producers on a run-of-the-play basis. An early hit, the now-forgotten *The Lion and the Mouse* (1905), ran for a record-breaking 686 performances. Most of the shows were booked by Daniel's brother Charles and included popular plays by the British writer J. M. Barrie. After Charles's death in 1915, Daniel joined forces with David Belasco in a series of respectable successes, including *The Gold Diggers* (1919) and the time-travel fantasy *Berkeley Square* (1929), starring Leslie Howard. After Belasco's death in 1930, Frohman continued on his own. He had some successes, notably Arthur Kober's comedy *Having Wonderful Time* (1937), but the continuing economic depression finally forced Frohman's departure in 1939. The Lyceum was saved from demolition by a consortium led by playwrights Kaufman and

2 Auditorium and proscenium, Lyceum Theatre, 1903

Hart, which bought the theatre and filled it with such hits as *Junior Miss* (1941) and *Born Yesterday* (1946). After Lee Shubert took over in 1949, the Lyceum continued its winning ways. British playwrights, including John Osborne (*Look Back in Anger*, 1957), Shelagh Delaney (*A Taste of Honey*, 1960), and Harold Pinter (*The Caretaker*, 1961), were among the featured attractions. The APA-Phoenix Repertory Company under the direction of Ellis Rabb leased the theatre (and Frohman's stock company infrastructure) from 1965 to 1969. The Shubert Organization came back in 1970, and the Lyceum has remained under its management. Recent memorable productions have included *Your Arms Too Short to Box With God* (1976) and *Master Harold . . . and the Boys* (1982).

1 Daniel Frohman's old Lyceum Theatre has the most finished and elaborate facade in the theatre district. The strong baroque columns, undulating marquee, and classic palladian windows brought a welcome lyricism to the staid brownstone fronts of turn-of-the-century 43rd Street. The theatre's lobby has mosaic tile floors, a vaulted ceiling, and lunette murals by James Wall Finn over the auditorium entrance.

2 A study in controlled contrasts, the Lyceum auditorium juxtaposes plain plaster walls with richly ornamented proscenium and box areas. The decor has the proper effect of drawing the theatregoer's eye inexorably toward the stage. Lighting fixtures are recessed into the ceiling in line with the architects' belief that chandeliers were a distraction to both audience and actors.

Lew Fields Theatre

254-58 West 42nd Street • Albert Edward Westover, Architect

Opened December 5, 1905; 880 seats • Reopened as Hackett Theatre, August 27, 1906

Oscar Hammerstein's final Times Square theatre project was the Lew M. Fields, named for half of the famous comedy team of Weber & Fields. Fields himself opened the theatre with a good run in Victor Herbert's *It Happened in Nordland* (1904). Unfortunately, the house itself turned out to be a flop; it was poorly planned and plagued by building code violations. The entrance and lobby were cramped, and the auditorium was unattractively decorated in the same pastry chef style used in Hammerstein's Theatre Republic. Oscar soon leased the house to the Shuberts, who promptly subleased to James Hackett, a prominent actor/producer. Hackett did well at first, notably with *The Chorus Lady* (1906) and a revival of *The Prisoner of Zenda* (1908). Meanwhile, Hammerstein sold the building to producer Henry Harris, who oversaw a major renovation in 1910 and renamed it the Harris Theatre. The interior was redesigned in a less flamboyant style and to accommodate the box office and the balcony entrance, which were removed from the sidewalk in the widening of 42nd Street. In the process, architects Herts & Tallant took out 14 proscenium boxes and several rows of seats. Yet another management team, the Selwyn brothers, took over in 1914 and used the theatre as a transfer house for aging hits that were attracting smaller but still profitable audiences. Producer Harry Frazee leased the theatre for *Wedding Bells*

(1919) and bought it one year later. He too renamed the house, Frazee Theatre. During his tenure Lynn Fontanne played her first starring role, in *Dulcy* (1921), and *Hell-Bent fer Heaven* (1924) won the Pulitzer Prize. Sublessee John Cort came in with another name change, Wallack's Theatre. He produced a hit, *Laff That Off* (1925), but then the theatre reverted to its losing ways, becoming a grind film house in 1930. As the rebuilt Anco Cinema, from 1940 to 1997 it was one of 42nd street's least-attractive movie houses. It was demolished as part of New York City's 42nd Street redevelopment.

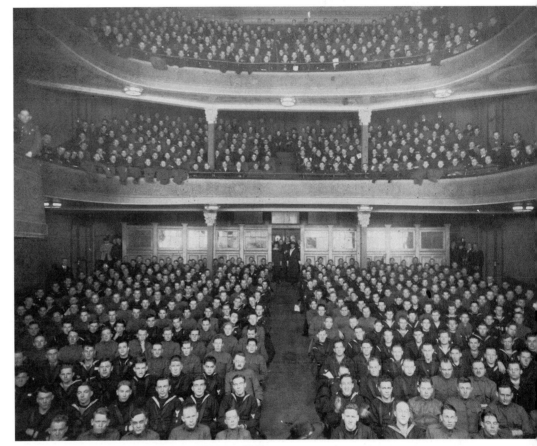

2 Auditorium, toward balconies, Harris Theatre, 1918

1 The original Fields marquee and front, with box office and balcony entrance on the sidewalk. The design of the facade is a modified Edwardian Baroque treatment of brick and limestone. To the right is the narrow entrance to the American Theatre and, on the corner, a bank.

2 During World War I the Harris hosted wartime vaudeville shows for U.S. servicemen. Renovations had stripped away most of Hammerstein's old architectural detail, but the center aisle and column-supported steep balconies were unchanged.

The Hippodrome

456-70 Sixth Avenue, 51-79 West 43rd Street, & 48-78 West 44th Street

Frederick Thompson and Jay H. Morgan, Architects • Opened April 12, 1905; 4678 seats

Promoted as the largest theatre in the world, the Hippodrome stands apart from other Broadway playhouses not only in its size but also in the scope of the mass audience spectaculars that were produced on its stage. The building was financed by the speculator John "Bet-A-Million" Gates and managed by Frederick Thompson and Elmer Dundy, who brought to Manhattan's new entertainment district the successful elements of their Coney Island fantasy, Luna Park. The two promoters aimed their bold and brassy entertainments at New York's huge working-class population. Backstage the Hippodrome was largely the creation of Claude Hagen, a prominent designer. Hagen was best known for the chariot race in *Ben-Hur* (1900), the spectacle that had drawn packed houses to the Broadway Theatre. Many of the scenic flats the producers planned to use were too massive to be be suspended in the loft. To solve this problem Hagen devised a series of deep "pockets," where sets could be stored before being rolled into position in full view of the audience. The most spectacular feature of the Hippodrome was its 200-

2 Hippodrome globe, 1905

foot-wide, 110-foot-deep stage, which could be moved up and down on hydraulic lifts. When the stage was lowered into a tank, it could be flooded with 400,000 gallons of water to become the scene of water ballets, mock sea battles, and other nautical novelties. The Hippodrome's opening show was *A Yankee Circus on Mars* (1905), rehashing a Luna Park mélange of music, ballet, and circus acts held together by a thin story line involving an interplanetary circus. This show and its successor, *A Society Circus* (1905), had good runs with two daily performances, but Dundy and Thompson failed to turn a profit. They were forced out, replaced by the Shuberts, who signed a ten-year lease. The brothers gave the audience everything it wanted and then some, from aerial dogfights in *Sporting Days* (1908) to the French Revolution (with guillotine) in *Wars of the World* (1914), but they kept costs in line and made money. The producer Charles Dillingham took over in 1915 and added celebrities such as John Philip Sousa and Harry Houdini to the bill. Dillingham moved on in 1923, and the Hippodrome was sold to the Keith-

1   The Hippodrome was built of steel and concrete faced with red brick and terra-cotta. On its exterior walls Classical details mingled with Moorish and other vaguely Eastern elements. The style was closely related to the facades of many pavilions at the World's Columbian Exposition in Chicago. In the foreground, the Sixth Avenue El ran by the building's entrance.

2   The Hippodrome framework globes atop towers on Sixth Avenue became famous New York landmarks. At night, when the globes and the rest of the building were outlined by thousands of stud electric bulbs, the Hippodrome was visible for miles around.

3   An arched central entrance led to a marble-lined box office lobby. Throughout the house bronze elephant heads served as lighting fixtures. The heads and another design motif, trios of charging horses, were allusions to the animals that were part of the Hippodrome's shows and to the ancient Greek sports arenas called *hippodromos*.

3   Box office lobby, Hippodrome, 1905

Albee interests. Architect Thomas Lamb redesigned the auditorium, eliminating the water tanks and creating a conventional (but still huge) vaudeville theatre, with a smaller proscenium opening within the framework of the old. Films were added to the bill in 1927, but the Hippodrome's days were numbered. Two years later the building was sold to real estate developers, who promptly ran out of money. The house remained dark until 1935, when showman Billy Rose opened the Rodgers & Hart circus spectacular *Jumbo*, starring Big Rosie in the title role and Jimmy Durante as the ringmaster. The show ran 233 performances but, like its early predecessors, lost money. The Hippodrome then saw intermittent use as an arena for various events before being demolished in 1939. The site is now occupied by an office building and a large parking garage.

4 Finale of *Neptune's Daughter*, 1907

5 Auditorium, renovated Hippodrome, 1923

4 The Hippodrome was known for its lavish, over-the-top productions. In 1906, the Shuberts astounded audiences with an effect they first produced for *Neptune's Daughter:* After finishing their final number, the chorus disappeared into the large pool of water in front of the stage. The secret became widely known—an underwater chamber partially filled with compressed air allowed performers to keep their heads above water as they walked out of sight—but the stunt remained popular and was repeated in subsequent productions.

5 For concerts the water tanks were covered to provide additional orchestra seats. There were about 2000 seats in the first balcony, 1450 in the second balcony, and about 1200 on the main floor.

Stuyvesant Theatre

111-21 West 44th Street • George Keister, Architect

Opened October 16, 1907; 1030 seats • Reopened as Belasco Theatre, September 3, 1910

Dramatist/impresario David Belasco put his firm imprint on the Stuyvesant Theatre as surely as if his name had been on the marquee from the outset. Known for his sumptuous, realistic productions, Belasco was intimately involved with every facet of his theatre. All of the equipment he installed—from Louis Hartman's complex lighting switchboard to the 10-by-18-foot elevator that brought up scenery and props from the basement shops—set the standard for modern theatrical design. Belasco's offices were in the west wing, and after 1910 he lived in a ten-room duplex apartment on top of the east wing. Despite often-cool critical reaction, audiences loved most of Belasco's productions. Among the theatre's early successes was *The Return of Peter Grimm* (1907), starring David Warfield. Belasco's star dimmed as popular tastes changed in the 1920s. But after his death in

1930, his theatre thrived under several managements. In the mid-1930s the Group Theatre put on a number of Clifford Odets plays, punctuated in 1935 by Sidney Kingsley's long-running *Dead End*. Familiar names such as *Johnny Belinda* (1940) and *Home of the Brave* (1945) played the Belasco before the Shuberts bought the property in 1948; the brothers soon leased it to NBC for use as a radio studio. After five years legitimate theatre returned with *The Solid Gold Cadillac* (1953) and a string of solid plays, including the Pulitzer Prize-winning *All the Way Home* (1960). In 1971 the popular sex farce *Oh! Calcutta* began its long run on Broadway, followed by a couple of hits transferred from other theatres—David Mamet's *American Buffalo* (1977) and the Fats Waller revue *Ain't Misbehavin'* (1981). Tony Randall's National Actors Theatre began at the Belasco in 1991.

2 Auditorium, Stuyvesant Theatre, 1907

3   David Belasco's studio, c. 1920

1   The handsome, well-proportioned facade of Belasco's playhouse was made of red brick with white terra-cotta detailing, designed in the neo-Georgian style more commonly found in mansions than in theatres. Three double-height Palladian windows are flanked by white pilasters and surmounted by a pediment containing a bullseye window. At the left, the west wing housed a lobby and offices. The entrance lobby and doors were designed by John Rapp.
(Photo on page 51)

2   The auditorium was comparatively shallow but was wide enough to accommodate about 1000 people. The rich walnut paneling, ornamental Tiffany lamps, and eighteen mural panels by Edward Shinn created a warm, comfortable setting for Belasco's standard mix of dazzling scenic effects and melodramatic hokum. Each of the ceiling panels held a domed lighting unit bearing the painted coat of arms of a person or place significant in theatrical history.

3   David Belasco's ten-room duplex apartment, above the east wing of the theatre, was reached by private elevator. Here the impresario lived and held court amid his collection of theatrical memorabilia and, reportedly, erotic art.

4   David Belasco was a pioneer in what has come to be known as environmental production, where the stage setting is extended to include the auditorium. Here both proscenium and auditorium have been redecorated for the theatre's production of *The Son-Daughter.*

4   Auditorium, Belasco Theatre, 1919

Manhattan Opera House

311-21 West 34th Street & 322-32 West 35th Street

J. B. McElfatrick & Son, Architects • Opened December 3, 1906; 3100 seats

◄ 1

The irrepressible Oscar Hammerstein realized a long-held ambition when he opened his greatest production, the Manhattan Opera House, as a rival to the Metropolitan Opera House. The Manhattan was on 34th Street, near the recently opened Pennsylvania Station, whereas the Met at 39th Street and Broadway was much closer to the burgeoning Times Square theatre district. Financed by Hammerstein's enormous profits from his Victoria Theatre, the new auditorium was a departure from the traditional horseshoe-shaped opera house. Although larger than the Met, the Manhattan appeared smaller and more intimate because the three deep balcony shelves occupied so much of the air space. In fact, half the seats were in the top two balconies, reflecting Oscar's desire to bring music to the masses. To improve acoustics throughout the house, a sounding board was installed just within the proscenium. Hammerstein brought to New York many modern European works that had been ignored by the Metropolitan. Between 1906 and 1911, he staged the American premieres of Charpentier's *Louise*, Debussy's *Pelleas et Melisande*, and Massenet's *Thais*. He also booked great singers like Nellie Melba, Luisa Tetrazzini, Mary Garden, and John McCormack. Income failed to meet expenses, and in 1911 Hammerstein was bought out by the capitalist and head of the rival Met, Otto Kahn, on the condition that Oscar stay clear of opera for ten years. The Shuberts leased the Manhattan from 1911 to 1917, using it as a cheap-ticket transfer and revival house. After Oscar died in 1919, the former opera house had a number of owners, including the Masons, who added a rooftop ballroom and a new 34th Street facade, both by architect Eugene DeRosa, in 1922. Beginning in 1927 Warner Brothers leased the space for use as a sound stage. The final entertainment tenant was a production of *The Eternal Road* (1937), an epic pageant of Jewish history for which director Max Reinhardt and designer Norman Bel Geddes gutted the auditorium, removing both the proscenium boxes and the arch itself. In 1940 the grand old theatre became a meeting hall, Manhattan Center, used mostly by unions, and then (in 1976) a warehouse.

2 House right, Manhattan Opera House, 1906

1 The facade of Oscar Hammerstein's Manhattan Opera House was faced in tan and white brick with brownstone trim. The formal portico and false cornice and pediment below the roofline did much to bring order and unity to the structure. The design indicated to some that architect McElfatrick was trying to shed his Victorian roots and come to terms with the Beaux Arts classicism becoming popular at the time.

2 With its gold leaf detailing, the auditorium was bolder and less restrained in its decoration than many theatres of the day. The plasterwork canopies above the proscenium boxes were particularly lush, with garlands, urns, and other decorative elements in glorious profusion. The balconies were supported by old-fashioned posts instead of cantilevers, thus leaving many in the audience with obstructed views.

Gaiety Theatre

1547 Broadway & 200-204 West 46th Street

Herts & Tallant, Architects • Opened August 30, 1908; 787 seats

The Gaiety Theatre was by built by Klaw & Erlanger as a home for the popular light comedy productions of George M. Cohan and his partner Sam Harris. Their early Gaiety shows included *The Fortune Hunter* (1909) and *Nearly Married* (1913). Other producers also booked shows into the theatre. Notable among their offerings were *Daddy Long-Legs* (1914) and *Turn to the Right!* (1916). The Gaiety's biggest success was *Lightnin'* (1918), the story of a charming, incorrigible liar, with the play's coauthor, Frank Bacon, in the title role. This show was the first on Broadway to run over 1000 performances. George Gershwin's *Tell Me More* (1925) was one of the last live productions at the Gaiety before it was converted to a movie house in 1926. (By the end of the 1920s, most of the Times Square theatres with entrances on Broadway had been converted.) In 1935, the Gaiety became one of Minsky's best-known burlesque houses, continuing to attract a large male audience until Mayor Fiorello H. LaGuardia's crackdown on skin shows in 1942. As the Victoria, the theatre once more became a movie house, and in 1949 it was renovated into one of the first intimate venues in Times Square for films marketed to specialized audiences. The name was changed to Embassy in 1980, but two years later the

2   Auditorium, Gaiety Theatre, 1908

old theatre was closed. The former "house of hits" and the neighboring Astor Theatre were the first of five playhouses demolished to provide a site for the Marriott Marquis Hotel and the adjoining 1600-seat Marquis Theatre.

1   The Gaiety's 46th Street facade, although not the theatre's main entrance, was an impressive design, rather like the architects' Brooklyn Academy of Music of the same period. The walls were of light gray Flemish bond brick with an elaborate terra-cotta cornice and window surrounds. The Broadway entrance was in a nondescript office building. From the early 1930s until demolition, both frontages were hidden behind massive billboards.

2   The small auditorium was finished in Louis XV style. The cupola-like proscenium boxes were supported by Composite order columns. Both box fronts and cornice bore a shell motif. On the original gray silk wall coverings were stylized comic masks beneath the interlocked initials G and T. The ceiling fixtures consisted of bare bulbs inset in an eight-pointed star pattern within the elaborate coffered panels.

3   All traces of the original Gaiety were obliterated in the 1949 renovation designed by architect Edward Durell Stone. He enlarged the auditorium to 1050 seats, extending it through the stage house, dropped the ceiling, and covered the walls with a sheathing of aluminum mesh screenwork.

◄ **3**   Renovated auditorium, Victoria Theatre, 1949

Maxine Elliott's Theatre

107-15 West 39th Street

Marshall & Fox, Architects • Opened December 30, 1908; 934 seats

An actress of exceptional beauty but modest ability, Maxine Elliott was a turn-of-the-century star whose celebrity was heightened by her reputed liaisons with rich and powerful men. She was also an astute businesswoman and a partner with Lee Shubert in this theatre, the first of many he and his brother J.J. built in the Times Square area. The "Venus de Milo with arms," as Ethel Barrymore called her, thus became the first actress since Laura Keene to build and manage a self-named theatre in the United States. Maxine Elliott's was one of the most lavishly designed theatres of its time. The backstage area had five tiers of dressing rooms, each carpeted and most with outside window and private lavatory. The performers had never been so pampered. Elliott herself had a three-room suite just off stage left. All of this carefully planned luxury did not bring much success to the house in its first decade. Of sixty productions, only four, including Edward Sheldon's most popular play, *Romance* (1912), achieved good runs. Maxine Elliott retired from the stage in 1920, after a farewell performance at her theatre as Cordelia in *Trimmed in Scarlet*, and moved to her villa on the Riviera. Under Shubert management the theatre's fortunes improved. Numerous successes included Jeanne Eagels' legendary portrayal of Sadie Thompson in *Rain* (1922), Helen Hayes' starring role in George Abbott's *Coquette* (1917), and Lillian Hellman's first hit as a playwright, *The Children's Hour* (1934). The Shuberts leased the aging house to the Federal Theatre Workshop in 1936 and to WOR-Mutual Radio in 1941. CBS took over the lease in 1944 and four years later began broadcasting Ed Sullivan's early TV show, *Toast of the Town*, from the Elliott stage. The theatre was demolished in 1956.

2   Auditorium, Maxine Elliott's Theatre, 1908

3   Orchestra promenade, Maxine Elliott's Theatre, 1908

1   Maxine Elliott's was the first New York theatre designed by the Chicago firm of Marshall & Fox. They modeled the chaste white Dover marble facade after the exterior of Le Petit Trianon in Versailles. Though the stage house was barely visible from the street, the architects had it sheathed in custom-molded white brick, raised in patterns to resemble a giant latticework trellis.

2   The Elliott auditorium was decorated in the Louis XIV style in shades of ivory and gold with light brown fabrics. Gold silk lined the side walls. A pair of marble Ionic columns flanked the proscenium, and balusters of the same material enclosed the orchestra-level boxes

3   The orchestra promenade was an elegant space separated from the auditorium by velvet curtains. Wall panels were of gold silk damask, and the ornamental relief ceiling was painted an ivory color. Stairs at each end of the promenade led down to lounges and up to the balcony.

New Theatre

21-29 Central Park West & 1-15 West 62nd Street • Carrere & Hastings, Architects

Opened November 6, 1909; 2318 seats • Reopened as Century Theatre, October 21, 1911

The New Theatre was conceived as the first American nonprofit theatre in the European tradition, dedicated to the presentation of classic and standard repertoire. The theatre was to be supported by private subscriptions, however, rather than government subsidies. To raise the $3 million needed to buy the land and build a grand playhouse, the wealthy founders of the New Theatre sold thirty private boxes for $100,000 each. Additional funds came from the sale of some orchestra seats for $3000 each. The "glorious temple to the drama" opened in 1909 to a barrage of criticism: poor acoustics, excessive distance between the stage and most seats (even the expensive boxes!), and overblown decorations throughout the house—a mere "plaything for the rich." Perhaps worst of all was the location, twenty blocks north of the booming Times Square theatre district. In the New Theatre's first season twelve productions ran only a few weeks each. The

poser himself singing "Oh, How I Hate to Get Up in the Morning." The Shuberts bought the theatre in 1920 for $1.25 million and expanded its seating capacity by almost 30 percent. Visiting companies, revivals

2 Auditorium, house right, New Theatre, 1909

theatre was redesigned for the second season, but to no avail. The millionaires folded their wallets and moved on, and the renamed Century Theatre was leased to Charles Dillingham and a succession of profit-minded managers. Diaghilev and his Ballet Russe were among the troupes booked into the Century, but popular musicals dominated the bill. Of particular note were Victor Herbert and Irving Berlin's *The Century Girl* (1916) and Berlin's classic all-soldier show *Yip! Yap! Yaphank* (1918), with the com-

of operettas like *The Chocolate Soldier*, and transfers of successful shows from other theatres were the standard fare, but the Century's most notable booking was Max Reinhardt's staging of *The Miracle* (1924), a religious pageant-play designed by Norman Bel Geddes. In 1930 the Shuberts traded the Century for three theatres on West 44th and 45th streets owned by Irwin and Henry Chanin, real estate developers. The Chanins demolished the theatre and built the 31-story Century Apartments on the site.

1 A pure expression of the architects' Beaux Arts training and professional beliefs, the New Theatre was clad entirely in Indiana limestone. Above the rusticated first story, Ionic pilasters flanked the triple-height windows. The doors were of bronze. In the rounded corner pavilions were circular staircases of white marble, leading to the first balcony and second story foyer.

2 In attempting to design an auditorium that would be suitable for both operas and plays, the architects created a hall that was not ideal for either art form. Providing space just behind the orchestra for the members' private boxes forced them to adopt a horseshoe-shaped design more suitable to the 19th century than to the 20th. The past was also echoed by the sumptuous decoration, which was heavily influenced by Louis XV's Court Theatre at Versailles. An expensive renovation within a year after this photo was taken kept most of the ornate plasterwork but changed the configuration of the seating.

3 Atop the New Theatre was a garden pavilion originally intended as a cafe. It was used briefly as a children's theatre and, from 1915-1920, was a Ziegfeld-managed cabaret designed by Joseph Urban. The Shuberts then transformed the roof into a 500-seat theatre and booked a variety of late-night revues. The most notable offering was *Chauve-Souris*, a kind of vaudeville performed in annual editions (1922–1925) by exiled members of the Russian Art Theatre. For these productions the hall was decorated with vibrant Slavic murals.

3 Rooftop playhouse, Century Theatre, 1922

4 Many critics faulted the New Theatre for its lavish interior decoration. Others were more selective. They found the U-shaped promenade surrounding the auditorium to be "elegant" in its Classical austerity. The marble walls and floor were certainly the equal of similar spaces in many European showplaces.

4 Promenade, New Theatre, 1909

Globe Theatre

1555 Broadway & 203-17 West 46th Street • Carrere & Hastings, Architects

Opened January 10, 1910; 1416 seats • Reopened as Lunt-Fontanne Theatre, May 5, 1958

The Globe Theatre opened to rave reviews as one of Broadway's most elegant and well-appointed playhouses. It was built for and managed by producer Charles Dillingham, one of the most admired figures in the theatre. He named the new playhouse for Shakespeare's theatre in London, but filled its stage with modern musicals. He booked works by Victor Herbert and Irving Berlin and by composers like Ivan Caryll, whose popularity has not endured. Many of these productions starred the popular comedian Fred Stone. The 1920s roared for Dillingham, with three editions of *George White's Scandals* (1920, 1922, 1923), all with songs by

2   Lunt-Fontanne Theatre, 46th Street facade, 1958

George Gershwin, and the decade's most popular musical, Vincent Youmans' *No, No Nanette* (1925). Sadly, Dillingham lost his fortune in the 1929 Crash. His beloved Globe was foreclosed and converted to a motion picture theatre in 1932. Thus it remained until Robert Dowling and the City Playhouses Group bought the theatre in 1957 and renamed it Lunt-Fontanne. The architectural firm of Roche & Roche was commissioned to design the remodeling. Among other improvements, they closed the Broadway entrance, installed a new box office vestibule, and reconfigured the auditorium into a single-balcony

"shoebox" house. The theatre opened, fittingly, with Alfred Lunt and Lynne Fontanne making their farewell Broadway appearance, in Frederick Durrenmatt's *The Visit* (1958). The theatre once more became one of Broadway's favored venues. Numbered among its hits are Rodgers and Hammerstein's *The Sound of Music* (1959), Neil Simon and Cy Coleman's *Little Me* (1962), the Duke Ellington musical *Sophisticated Ladies* (1981), and *Titanic* (1997). The Nederlander organization purchased the theatre in 1973 and still owns it today.

1   The Broadway entrance to the Globe was built into an old brownstone house. The facade was narrow but, with its Ionic pilasters and sophisticated signs, suitable for the carriage (and limousine) trade.
(Photo on previous page)

2   The 46th Street facade of the Globe was little changed after the theatre's rebirth as the Lunt-Fontanne. This 1958 photo shows the original five-bay central pavilion topped by an elaborate overhanging cornice and red tile roof. Each bay contains a double-height arched window surmounted by a terra-cotta cartouche with a pair of reclining nudes holding the traditional masks of Comedy and Tragedy. Just above the new, electroplated bronze and glass marquee, the old sculpted heads continue to look down on the audience entering the theatre.

3 Mezzanine lounge, Lunt-Fontanne Theatre, 1958

3 The complete remodeling of the theatre's interior in 1958 left very little of
the old Globe. Among the important
additions was an elegant lounge at the
mezzanine level, its walls decorated
with paneled mirrors and murals of
European opera houses.

4 The Globe's original auditorium
exhibited much the same Beaux Arts
inspiration as the theatre's exterior.
Six proscenium boxes flanked either
side of the stage; those at the balcony
level were swathed in rose-colored
draperies. Above, a coved ceiling rose
to a central panel, painted to resemble
a skyscape, that could be opened in fair
weather. The shallow, fan-shaped seating allowed for greater intimacy
between players and audience.

◄ 4 Auditorium, Globe Theatre, 1910

George M. Cohan's Theatre

1482 Broadway & 142-54 West 43rd Street

George Keister, Architect • Opened February 13, 1911; 1086 seats

2   Proscenium boxes and stage right, George M. Cohan's Theatre, 1911

George M. Cohan, the quintessential song-and-dance man, was also a playwright, director, producer, and, with the opening of his own theatre on Broadway, owner-manager as well. George and his producing partner Sam Harris were also partners in the theatre. Cohan and his shows were more beloved by audiences than by theatrical critics or intellectuals, and his theatre was virtually a shrine to his career as a "people's performer." In the marble-lined lobby the vaudeville years of the Four Cohans were illustrated, from George's stage debut with his family at age nine to their appearance in *The Governor's Son* (1901), the first full-length musical comedy George ever wrote. Scenes from George's greatest stage successes were depicted in murals over the boxes. The opening-night audience was enthusiastic about these decorations as well as the play on stage—George's *Get-Rich-Quick Wallingford*, a hit transferred from the Gaiety Theatre. Other Cohan productions came and went at the the-atre, as did a number of shows, like the popular *Potash and Perlmutter* (1913), put on by others. Cohan and Harris sold the theatre to their neighbor Joe Leblang, the famed discount ticket agent, in 1915 and dissolved their partnership in 1920. The theatre's management was then turned over to A. L. Erlanger. During his tenure Ed Wynn's performance in *The Perfect Fool* (1921) was notable, as was the transfer of Eugene O'Neill's *Desire Under the Elms* from the much larger Earl Carroll in 1925 and the opening of the musical *Rain or Shine* in 1928. But in between live performances some silent films were booked. Paramount's *The Ten Commandments* (1923) and M-G-M's *Ben-Hur* (1925) were major moneymakers. In 1932 George M. Cohan's Theatre became a full-time film house. After Leblang defaulted on his mortgages in 1938, the prematurely aging theatre and the neighboring Fitzgerald Building were demolished.

1   The Broadway marquee and narrow entrance to George M. Cohan's Theatre were part of the Fitzgerald Building, a commonplace office tower. From this portal a long corridor led to the lobby and auditorium on 43rd Street. There was a wider entrance on that street, its white terra-cotta facade vaguely Renaissance in derivation. In the vaulted, marble-lined lobby, murals illustrated the vaudeville years of the Four Cohans.

2   Intricate plasterwork in the style of the Italian Renaissance decorated the proscenium boxes and arch. Murals just below the ceiling illustrated George M. Cohan's life in the theatre.

3   The auditorium of George M. Cohan's Theatre was lavishly finished with gray marble wainscoting. Elaborate ceiling coffers and bronze chandeliers added to the theatre's elegant ambiance. The old-fashioned columns supporting the balconies obstructed the view from a number of seats.

3   Auditorium, George M. Cohan's Theatre, 1911

The Winter Garden

1634-46 Broadway, 762-76 Seventh Avenue, & 201-209 West 50th Street

William Albert Swasey, Architect • Opened March 20, 1911; 1533 seats

The venerable Winter Garden traces its origins to the American Horse Exchange (1885), owned by a syndicate headed by the millionaire William K. Vanderbilt. With the decline of the horse in New York, and with the transformation of Times Square into the city's new entertainment district, Vanderbilt leased this large property to the Shuberts in 1910. The brothers quickly had the building converted into a theatre, cafe, and restaurant. Al Jolson made his Broadway debut at the theatre in 1911 and performed there regularly until 1925, when he migrated to Hollywood. Another mainstay of the Winter Garden bill was the Shuberts' annual revue, *The Passing Show* (1912–1924). Three of

Olsen & Johnson's madcap hit comedies, including *Hellzapoppin* (1938), also played the theatre. Like many Broadway playhouses, the Winter Garden sometimes has been used as a motion picture palace (1928–33; 1945–48). Since 1950, however, musical comedies—most of them long-running hits—have dominated the Garden's bill. A short list includes *Wonderful Town* (1953), *West Side Story* (1957), *Funny Girl* (1964), *Pacific Overtures* (1976), and *42nd Street* (1980). The auditorium was renovated in 1980, but in two years the new decor was covered over by the all-encompassing scenery for the phenomenal *Cats*, the longest-running show in Broadway history.

2 Auditorium, Winter Garden, 1911

1 The conversion of the American Horse Exchange into the Winter Garden Theatre involved comparatively little work on the exterior. Architect William A. Swasey retained the basic lines of the old arena, while adding a Georgian-inspired graystone front with pressed metal cornice and pediment and a rooftop cupola. This new facade and the relatively small entrance to the Winter Garden were placed in the middle of the block, enabling the Shuberts to rent most of the Broadway frontage to retail stores. In addition, they built a three-story nightclub space on the (near) corner

of 50th Street and Broadway. The location flourished under many names, including Palais de Danse, Montmartre, Singapore, and others.

2 With its exposed, light-bulb-studded beams and roof painted with scenes of landscape and sky, the theatre recreated the ambiance of the outdoor roof gardens then popular on Broadway. Reflecting its origins, however, the theatre was found by many to be cold and barnlike . . . with poor acoustics to boot.

3 In 1922 the Shuberts engaged Herbert Krapp to modernize the auditorium. He lowered the ceiling and decorated the house in red and gold with an amalgam of Adamesque and 18th-century French styles. Krapp also reduced the proscenium width through the use of drapes and a false inner arch. A large plaster fresco, "The Shepherd's Dream," was installed on the sounding board.

3 Proscenium, Winter Garden, 1923

4 Renovated auditorium, Winter Garden, 1923

4 The new theatre was decidedly warmer, with a more intimate feeling than the former imitation roof garden. Some patrons were dismayed, however, to see that 100 new seats had replaced the famous runway, on which the Shuberts' well-advertised "Beauty Brigade of Bewitching Broadway Blondes and Brunettes" had enlivened most shows by parading from the stage to the last row of orchestra seats.

Folies Bergere

206-14 West 46th Street • Herts & Tallant, Architects

Opened April 27, 1911; 636 seats at tables • Reopened as Fulton Theatre, October 20, 1911; 895 seats

◄ 1

2 Proscenium, Folies Bergere, 1911

Opening a theatre restaurant in New York based on the popular Parisian nightspot seemed like a good idea to producers Henry B. Harris and Jesse L. Lasky. But the Folies Bergere soon proved to be a magnificent flop, closing its doors just months after opening, then converting to a playhouse of conventional layout. Nor did this new theatre, renamed the Fulton, do much to light up Broadway. Only three shows—including *The Misleading Lady* with Lewis Stone—ran longer than 150 performances before A. L. Erlanger took over management of the theatre in 1921. His tenure was enlivened with several Theatre Guild shows transferred from the Garrick and with Bela Lugosi's signature interpretation of *Dracula* (1927). Erlanger's death in 1930 and the onset of the Depression brought a dry spell to the Fulton until an intimate revue,

1   The facade of the Folies Bergeres was a unique lacy diamond weave of cream, red, and blue terra-cotta tile. At the top, under an ornate bronze cornice of alternating comic masks and torchéres, was an allegorical mural by William DeLeftwich Dodge, "Vaudeville Paying Homage to Les Folies-Bergères." On the roof electric signs in the shape of hanging banners flashed the theatre's name.
(Photo on previous page)

2   The theatre-restaurant's proscenium was picture-perfect, crowned by two trumpeting angels and a portrait of a Parisian beauty. Flanking the proscenium were two murals, again by Dodge, of pastoral scenes derived from Watteau. (The murals were painted over by Joseph Urban in his redesign of the theatre for A. L. Erlanger in the 1920s.)

3   French Rococo was the predominant style of the Folies Bergere, with a suggestion of the pastoral in the plaster latticework and fruit swags throughout. Tables and chairs took up the entire orchestra and front tier of the balcony. Many Frenchmen were on the restaurant's staff, both in the theatre and in the kitchen beneath the stage.

4   In 1958 the Helen Hayes was extensively refurbished. A new facade-length marquee was installed, and the interior decor was simplified and painted a uniform beige. Nevertheless, as seen in this photograph, a lot of the old elegance was preserved amidst the modern stage lights.

3   Restaurant and balconies, Folies Bergere, 1911

New Faces (1934) caught the public's fancy. The enduring *Arsenic and Old Lace* opened at the Fulton in 1941 and ran for 1444 performances. In 1955 the Fulton was renamed the Helen Hayes Theatre, in honor of "the first lady of the American stage." The theatre booked a number of distinguished plays, including Eugene O'Neill's *Long Day's Journey into Night* (1956) and *A Touch of the Poet* (1958), Jean Kerr's *Mary, Mary* (1961), *6 Rooms Riv Vu* (1972), and a revival of Kaufman and Ferber's *The Royal Family* (1975). During this period the Helen Hayes became the center of controversy. Along with five neighboring theatres, it was slated to be replaced by a skyscraper hotel as part of the redevelopment of Times Square. The battle between developers and preservationists lasted a decade, but in 1982 the old theatres were torn down—and in 1983 the Little Theatre, on 44th Street, was renamed the Helen Hayes.

4 Auditorium, Helen Hayes Theatre

The Playhouse

137-45 West 48th Street

Charles Alonzo Rich, Architect • Opened April 15, 1911; 863 seats

Producer William A. Brady built, owned, and operated The Playhouse until he retired and sold the house to the Shuberts in 1944. Manager of theatrical stars such as Tallulah Bankhead, Laurette Taylor, and his wife, Grace George, Brady also produced over 250 plays in New York. He kept The Playhouse going with hits like George Broadhurst's *Bought and Paid For* (1911), distinguished productions like G. B. Shaw's *Major Barbara* (U.S. premiere 1915), and a host of other plays, good and bad. After Brady produced Elmer Rice's Pulitzer Prize-winning hit *Street Scene* at The Playhouse in 1929, both he and the theatre endured a number of flops before *Three Men on a Horse* came to the rescue in 1935. Under Shubert management in the 1940s and '50s The Playhouse did better than most theatres east of Broadway. Tennessee Williams' *The Glass Menagerie* (1945) and William Gibson's *The Miracle Worker* (1959) both drew large audiences. But, in the end, the inconvenient location finished The Playhouse. It was demolished in 1969 to make way for an expansion of Rockefeller Center.

2 Auditorium, The Playhouse, 1911

1 The facade of The Playhouse was a handsome, restrained neo-Georgian creation of red brick trimmed with limestone. Stone carvings of Tragedy and Comedy were set into the wall. The steel-and-glass canopy was flanked by brick posts joined by an iron fence. William Brady's production offices and a rehearsal hall occupied the top two floors, tucked under the green copper mansard roof.

2 The two-balcony Playhouse was shallow, contributing to an intimacy between performers and audience. The extra-large width, however, provided sufficient seating capacity to enable the theatre to pay its way over the years. Decoration was conservative: The predominant colors were dark red and gold, with brown carpeting and blue draperies.

Little Theatre

238-44 West 44th Street • Ingalls & Hoffman, Architects

Opened March 12, 1912; 299 seats • Reopened as Helen Hayes Theatre, July 12, 1983

When Winthrop Ames was dismissed as manager of the grandiose but ill-fated New Theatre, he built a playhouse that was small, and almost unadorned—the antithesis of the New. Unfortunately, in its early years the Little was not a commercial success though it did offer several notable productions. Austrian playwright Arthur Schnitzler's first success, *Anatol* (1912), with John Barrymore in the title role, played the Little, as did G. B. Shaw's *The Philanderer* (1913). The Little's financial health improved after Architect Herbert J. Krapp's redesign increased the seating and improved the acoustics in 1920. A comedy, *Pigs* (1924),

2   Original auditorium, Little Theatre, 1912

ran for almost a year, as did *2 Girls Wanted* (1926). Winthrop Ames retired in 1931 and sold the Little to his neighbor, The New York Times Company. Persuaded not to demolish the building, the Times leased the theatre to CBS Radio and to various producers, then used it as a venue for lectures and concerts under the name New York Times Hall from 1941 until 1959. Thereafter, the theatre was leased to ABC Television (1969-1963) and Westinghouse Broadcasting (1965-1974), with a brief interruption for several runs of legitimate theatre, including *Tambourines to Glory* (1963) and *The Subject Was Roses* (1964). Among later notable productions at the new Little were *Gemini* (1977) and *Torch Song Trilogy* (1982). The theatre was renamed for Helen Hayes in 1983. *Prelude to a Kiss* opened at the Hayes in 1990.

3   Lounge and tearoom, Little Theatre, 1912

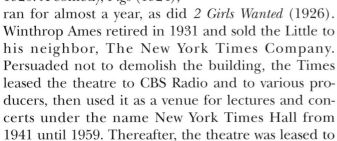

1   The Little Theatre's refined Georgian Revival facade, with its delicate white trim and handsome window shutters, suggests a Boston townhouse more than a Times Square theatre. The box office lobby was in the same mode, paneled in white-painted pine.

2   The original auditorium of the Little Theatre was small but not cramped, with just 299 seats on one level. The walls had dark-brown birch wainscotting below reproductions of Boucher tapestries. The wood paneling was removed in the 1917 renovation, when a balcony was added, thus increasing the seats to 499, and the house was reconfigured on a more conventional fan-shaped plan.

3   The intimate feeling of the theatre was carried over into the tearoom on the lower level. The room was paneled in wood and furnished with Jacobean reproductions.

Eltinge 42nd Street Theatre

236-42 West 42nd Street

Thomas White Lamb, Architect • Opened September 11, 1912; 880 seats

The Eltinge was built by impresario Al Woods as a home for the lurid melodramas and bedroom farces that had made him one of Broadway's most successful producers. Woods named the theatre for one of his most popular stars, the female impersonator Julian Eltinge. Another star of the time, Jane Cowl, opened the Eltinge with her performance in Bayard Veiller's melodrama *Within the Law* (1912) The show ran for a year and a half and was followed by other hits, including *The Yellow Ticket* (1914), with John Barrymore, and *Fair and Warmer* (1915), the first of many popular farces to play the Eltinge. Both Woods and his theatre declined in the 1920's—the last notable production was *Blackbirds of 1928*—and the Eltinge became a burlesque house in 1931. In 1941 the renamed Laffmovie began showing Hollywood comedies, and in 1954 the old Eltinge took on another new name, Empire. In perhaps the most dramatic move of its career, in 1998 the building was transported to a new foundation 200 feet to the west on 42nd Street. As part of New York's redevelopment of the theatre district, Al Woods' lobby will be restored as the grand entrance to a new 25-screen motion picture theatre.

1   The 42nd Street facade of the Eltinge Theatre was a terra-cotta replication of a Roman triumphal arch, widened slightly to accommodate the theatre's entrance and a large window that flooded the box office lobby with light. The marquee was of steel and glass. In fair weather, manager Al Woods often came down from his office under the theatre's mansard roof and sat in front of his playhouse, greeting patrons with a familiar "Hello, sweetheart."

2   A rather small house, the Eltinge gave the illusion of being large through its steeply inclined side walls that rose to a central ceiling dome. The decor was an eclectic mix of ancient Greek and Egyptian motifs, the latter displayed in a winged disk and paired sphinxes above the proscenium arch. A mural on the sounding board depicted a trio of Grecian maidens dancing to the music of Pan.

2   Auditorium, Eltinge Theatre, 1912

Weber & Fields' Music Hall

216-32 West 44th Steet • William Albert Swasey, Architect

Opened November 21, 1912; 1468 seats • Reopened as 44th Street Theatre, December 29, 1913

The Shuberts' named their first theatre on 44th Street for two popular comedians of the day, Joe Weber and Lew Fields. But two months after the duo opened their theatre with a double bill of *Roly-Poly* and *Without the Law*, they broke up their act and never again appeared together on the New York stage. In late 1913 the Shuberts renamed their house the 44th Street Theatre. The roof garden was also renamed several times. Nora Bayes Theatre is the name most theatregoers associate with the place, which never achieved success. In the basement, the original rathskeller became the Little Club during Prohibition and the Stage Door Canteen during World War II. During its first two decades, the main auditorium was home to a variety of attractions—operettas by the likes of Rudolf Friml and Sigmund Romberg, Shubert-produced vaudeville, films, and the Marx Brothers' hit comedy *Animal Crackers* (1928). The 44th Street survived the Depression of the 1930s and had its biggest hits in the early 1940s: *Rosalinda* (1942), Moss Hart's *Winged Victory* (1943), and *Follow the Girls* (1944). The New York Times, which had

2 Rofftop auditorium, Nora Bayes Theatre, 1918

bought the property in 1940, demolished it in 1945 to provide space for a postwar expansion of its headquarters and printing plant.

3 Proscenium boxes, house right, Weber & Fields' Music Hall, 1913

1 The exterior of Weber & Fields' Music Hall was built of white brick and terra-cotta with a large expanse of paned windows just under the roof. Overall, the space devoted to the glassed-in roof garden gave the theatre a top-heavy look. The wall was divided into panels separated by Ionic pilasters and surmounted by Georgian-derived false pediments. A fire escape sloping across the front overpowered any attempt at architectural coherence.

2 As originally designed, Lew Fields' 44th Street Roof Garden was a large barren space with an open-beamed ceiling that made for poor acoustics. In 1917 the Shuberts engaged Herbert Krapp to redesign the space into a conventional theatre, with false walls and ceiling to improve the sound.

3 Stylistically, the auditorium exhibited the architect's predilection for 18th-century Georgian, providing a chaste, Classical setting for the raucous, Edwardian entertainment on stage. The Music Hall's decor was dominated by pilasters, swags, medallions, and panel latticework.

Cort Theatre

138-46 West 48th Street

Thomas White Lamb, Architect • Opened December 20, 1912; 999 seats

Vaudeville mogul turned theatrical producer John Cort built his New York headquarters theatre on 48th Street, east of Broadway. The area became known as "the street of hits" after the Cort and four other theatres became "lucky" houses. The Cort opened with a hit, *Peg o' My Heart* starring Laurette Taylor, and continued with such long-running productions as *Merton of the Movies* (1922) and Ferenc Molnar's *The Swan* (1923), with Eva LeGallienne. John Cort retired in 1927, and the theatre was leased to the Shuberts. They had success with many productions, including *Boy Meets Girl* (1935), *Room Service* (1937), *The Male Animal* (1940), and two Pulitzer Prize-winners, *The Shrike* (1952), starring Jose Ferrer, and *The Diary of Anne Frank* (1955). The Cort was used by a television hit, the Merv Griffin Show, from 1969 to 1972, and in 1974 Doug Henning's *The Magic Show* opened its four-and-one-half-year run. Among the stars who have appeared at the Cort are Ralph Bellamy (in *Sunrise at Campobello*, 1958), Robert Redford, Katharine Hepburn, Katharine Cornell, Marlon Brando, and Laurence Olivier.

2   Proscenium boxes and auditorium, Cort Theatre, 1912

3   Box office vestibule, Cort theatre, 1987

1   The Cort's chaste white marble front, like the exterior of Maxine Elliott's Theatre, was derived from Marie Antoinette's Le Petit Trianon at Versailles. Critics found the Cort's design freer in spirit, and judged its facade one of New York's most handsome.

2   Originally painted ivory and rose with dull gold relief, the Cort auditorium featured a sounding board mural by Arthur Brounet in the manner of Watteau and a lattice-work proscenium frame over backlit amber glass. A Wurlitzer Hope-Jones organ complemented the usual pit orchestra.

3   Within the Cort, the box office lobby is wainscotted in Pavanozza marble and has in one corner a bust of Marie Antoinette, after an original by Houdon. At its opening the lobby was embellished with bronze figures crafted by Tiffany Studios.

Princess Theatre

104-106 West 39th Street

William Albert Swasey, Architect • Opened March 14, 1913; 299 seats

2 Auditorium, Princess Theatre, 1913

The Princess Theatre was initally intended as an intimate house for one-act plays presented by a resident company—a classic "little theatre." A joint venture of the Shuberts and producer F. Ray Comstock, the Princess failed to live up to its promise during its first two years. Comstock was then persuaded to switch his format to offer intimate musicals with small casts and minimal sets—a refreshing contrast to the big productions dominating the Times Square scene just a few blocks north. Composer Jerome Kern and librettist Guy Bolton hit on the right formula with their second production for Comstock, *Very Good Eddie* (1916). British humorist P. G. Wodehouse then joined the team, which wrote three more celebrated Princess Theatre Musicals—*Oh, Boy!* (1917), *Leave It to Jane* (1917), and *Oh, Lady! Lady!* (1918). Theirs was

a tough act to follow, but Comstock tried hard, with Eugene O'Neill's *Emperor Jones* (1921) and Luigi Pirandello's *Six Characters in Search of an Author* (1922). During the rest of the 1920s production after production left a mediocre to poor record. Finally, in 1933, films filled the bill. That same year the Shuberts sold the house to the International Ladies Garment Workers' Union (ILGWU), which at first used the small space as a recreation center for all its members working in the neighborhood. As the renamed Labor Stage the theatre gave birth to the famous musical by and for union members, *Pins and Needles* (1937), which ran for 1108 performances. The Princess closed out its life under various names as a showcase for foreign films from 1947 until 1955, when it was demolished.

1 A simple red brick exterior with limestone trim, exhibiting the architect's fondness for the English Georgian style, gave the Princess more the look of a small office building than a theatre. Indeed, the five stories of rental office space helped the owners keep their books in the black, especially in the beginning.

2 The graceful blue-and-white Princess auditorium may be architect Swasey's most successful theatre interior. With only fourteen rows of seats, arranged off a center aisle, supplemented by twelve proscenium and mezzanine boxes, the theatre had good acoustics and audience sight lines. The decor freely mixed Georgian and French elements, notably in the Aubusson-inspired tapestries on both sides of the house.

Sam S. Shubert Theatre

221-33 West 44th Street

Office of Henry B. Herts, Architects • Opened September 29, 1913; 1391 seats

After the unsuccessful beginning of its large playhouse on West 61st Street, the board of the nonprofit New Theatre announced plans to move downtown. This time they wanted to build a smaller playhouse just off Times Square, on land owned by the Astor Estate. Financial problems forced the nonprofit theatre to withdraw, however, and the Shuberts won a lease on the property. Ultimately, they built four theatres on the site. On the corner of what came to be called Shubert Alley and 44th Street, the Sam S. Shubert Theatre was the first to be built. As the Shuberts' New York flagship, it was also Lee and J.J.'s memorial to their brother Sam, who had died in a train crash in 1905. The Shubert was a large theatre, made for the musicals popular at the time. (The neighboring Booth was warm and intimate, suitable for small-scale dramas. Among the Shubert's early hits were

2 Auditorium, Shubert Theatre, 1913

Sigmund Romberg's *Maytime* (1917), which ran for over a year, and six annual editions of *The Greenwich Village Follies* (1920-1925). The theatre's first Pulitzer Prize-winner, however, was a straight play—Robert E. Sherwood's *Idiot's Delight* (1936). Works created by Rodgers & Hart, Rodgers & Hammerstein, Cole Porter, Lerner & Loewe, Stephen Sondheim, and other icons of the musical theatre also appeared on the Shubert's stage, but the theatre's biggest hit was the Pulitzer Prize-winning *A Chorus Line.* Created by the choreographer Michael Bennett at Joseph Papp's Public Theatre, the show transferred to the Shubert in 1975 and ran for a record-breaking 6137 performances (surpassed only by *Cats,* in 1997).

1 The facades of both the Shubert Theatre and the neighboring Booth are of glazed white brick with terra-cotta rustication, in an Italian Renaissance style. Bands of plaster frescoes called sgraffito—a technique of etching plaster while it is still wet—are the principal decorative feature. The building housed two stories of Shubert offices and an apartment for brother Lee at the top.

2 Originally, the plaster walls of the Shubert auditorium were painted to resemble stonework with a richly detailed ornamental cornice. The house was lighted primarily by six bronze and crystal chandeliers. Subsequent redecorating has seen the walls covered in yellow imitation silk, but much of the original detailing remains, including panels painted by J. Mortimer Lichtenauer to represent various classical figures.

3 The exterior of the Shubert Theatre has changed little over the years. The illuminated sign for *A Chorus Line* became something of a Broadway institution, remaining on the corner for fifteen years. This photo shows the unornamented stage house facade at the right.

3 Exterior, Shubert Theatre, 1982

Booth Theatre

222-32 West 45th Street

Office of Henry B. Herts, Architects • Opened October 16, 1913; 704 seats

Just seventeen days after the Shubert Theatre opened, its fraternal twin and Shubert Alley neighbor on 45th Street presented its first production, Arnold Bennett's *The Great Adventure*. The new theatre was named for the actor Edwin Booth and was managed by Winthrop Ames. Comedies and drawing room dramas, especially imports from across the Atlantic, were favored at the Booth. G. B. Shaw's *Getting Married* (1916), A. A. Milne's *The Truth About Blayds* (1922), and John Galsworthy's *Escape* (1927) were typical offerings. In 1924 Alfred Lunt and Lynne Fontanne made their acting debut as a couple in *The Guardsman*. Winthrop Ames retired in 1932, and the Shuberts took over management of the Booth. Sixteen years later, in 1948, the Shuberts became landlords as well, buying from the Astor Estate the land on which the Booth, Shubert, Plymouth, and Broadhurst theatres were built. To date, the Booth has housed four winners of the Pulitzer Prize: Kaufman and Hart's *You Can't Take It With You* (1936), Saroyan's *The Time of Your Life* (1939), Jason Miller's *That Championship Season* (1972), and Sondheim's *Sunday in the Park With George* (1984). Adding more lustre to the Booth's record are dozens of memorable productions, including *Blithe Spirit* (1942), *Come Back, Little Sheba* (1950), *A Taste of Honey* (1960), *For Colored Girls ...* (1976), and *Mass Appeal* (1981). In 1979 interior designer Melanie Kahane designed a restoration of the Booth to its original elegance.

2   Auditorium toward boxes, house left, Booth Theatre, 1913

1   The Booth was smaller than the adjacent Shubert, from which it was separated by a thick fire wall running the height and breadth of the stage house. On the facade is a balustrade instead of the windows lighting the Shuberts' offices. Both theatres had rounded entrances on the corner of Shubert Alley.

2   The Booth holds only about half the number of seats in the Shubert but has about twice the larger theatre's lobby and lounge space. Tudor-Jacobean in style, the theatre had wooden wainscotting two thirds up the side walls. Above, three sets of false French windows were paned in mirrored glass. The ceiling is coved and contains four chandeliers, Empire in style.

3   The Booth's decor reflected the taste of manager Winthrop Ames, rather than that of the Shuberts. Over the years the interior was changed to reflect a more utilitarian approach to theatre design.

4   One of the reasons audiences found the Booth a pleasant place to spend an evening was the generous space given over to lobbies and lounges. The tearoom on the lower level looks much the same today as it did on the theatre's opening.

3   Auditorium, toward house right, Booth Theatre, 1913

4   Tearoom, lower level, Booth Theatre

Palace Theatre

1564-66 Broadway & 154-66 West 47th Street

Kirchoff & Rose, Architects • Opened March 24, 1913; 1736 seats

The Palace opened as a vaudeville house, flagship of the Keith-Albee circuit. The origin of the big theatre, however, was in the Orpheum circuit, which was strong west of Chicago but needed a presence in the key New York market. The Palace ran into trouble at first, when the powerful E. F. Albee let it be known that any performer who appeared at the Palace would be banished from the lucrative K-A circuit. Martin Beck, head of Orpheum, was forced to capitulate. After much wrangling, he ceded 75 percent ownership of the Palace to Albee but kept control of booking the acts. Beck's credibility soared when he persuaded Sarah Bernhardt to make her

2   Proscenium and boxes, Palace Theatre, 1913

first appearance on a vaudeville stage. She was an immediate hit, and the Palace became known as the top variety house in the world. All the stars appeared at the theatre—Lillian Russell, Ethel Barrymore, Will Rogers, Bojangles Robinson, W. C. Fields, et al—along with acts like "Odiva the Plunging Samoan Nymph," who performed water ballets with a corps of sea lions. Two daily shows of a nine-act bill was standard fare at the Palace, until dwindling box office receipts forced a third performance in 1929, then a fourth, and then a

3   Box office lobby, Palace Theatre, 1913

1   The Broadway facade of the Palace Theatre is another example of the Beaux Arts style adapted to a multi-use commercial building. Faced with white marble and terra-cotta detailing, the 12-story office building and theatre bore more than a passing resemblance to Herts & Tallant's New Amsterdam Theatre (1903). *(Photo on previous page)*

2   The original Palace auditorium was decorated with lavish ornamental plasterwork. Eighteen tiered boxes were arrayed along the side walls, in addition to ten loge boxes on each side of the orchestra.

3   From its opening, the Palace was known as the "Valhalla of Vaudeville," the pinnacle of achievement in the glamorous, now-vanished world of the variety artist. The outer lobby was a fitting entrance to this theatrical monument, decorated as it was in a variety of marbles and bronze fittings. Five pairs of double doors opened onto the grand inner lobby and a palatial staircase that led to the balcony.

fifth, with a motion picture thrown in. Variety was dropped altogether in 1935. Its prosperity renewed, the Palace did well through the 1940s, then languished until 1965, when it was purchased by the Nederlander Organization. Designer Ralph Alswang oversaw a major renovation, redecorating the house and rebuilding the stage to make the Palace suitable for legitimate theatre. Along with Judy Garland's memorable one-woman show in 1967, the Palace booked a number of hit musicals, including *Sweet Charity* (1966) with Gwen Verdon, *George M.* (1968) with Joel Grey, and Lauren Bacall in *Applause* (1970) and *Woman of the Year* (1981). *La Cage Aux Folles* (1983) ran for four and one-half years, and then the Palace was closed for a major construction project: Its old office building was replaced by the skyscraper Embassy Suites Hotel. The auditorium was again renovated, and a new entrance and Broadway marquee were designed by architects Fox & Fowle. *The Will Rogers Follies* ran for 983 performances beginning in 1991, followed by the stage version of Walt Disney's *Beauty and the Beast* (1994), which is still running today.

4 Palace Theatre entrance, Embassy Suites Hotel, 1991

4 In the Times Square of the 1990s hotels and theatres coexisted in an uneasy but commercially successful relationship. In the Palace auditorium hit shows continued to flourish, even though the venerable theatre was buried under a skyscraper and almost obliterated by billboards.

5 The Palace's well-planned sightlines and good acoustics created an intimacy between audiences and performers that was unusual in such a large space. The stage itself was smaller than some, with an impressive high proscenium arch.

5 Auditorium, Palace Theatre, 1913

Longacre Theatre

220-28 West 48th Street

Office of Henry Herts, Architect • Opened May 1, 1913; 1005 seats

Harry Frazee, a theatrical manager and promoter who also owned the Boston Red Sox, financed and built the Longacre Theatre in 1913. In Frazee's early years at the Longacre he produced some modestly successful plays, including *A Pair of Sixes* (1914) and *Nothing But the Truth* (1916). But in 1919, needing cash, he sold the Longacre to the Shuberts. (The next year he sold his contract with Babe Ruth to the New York Yankees.) The Shuberts didn't do as well on their Frazee deal as the Yankees did on theirs, but they did have some successful bookings—George S. Kaufman's *The Butter and Egg Man* (1925), Patrick Kearney's dramatization of Dreiser's *An American Tragedy* (1926), and the Clifford Odets double bill, *Till the Day I Die* and *Waiting for Lefty* (1935). The theatre then languished until 1943, when the Shuberts leased it to WOR Radio Mutual for use as a studio. It returned to the ranks of legitimate theatres with Robert Preston in *The Tender Trap* (1954). Later successes included *Purlie Victorious* (1961), the Fats Waller revue *Ain't Misbehavin'* (1978), and *Children of a Lesser God* (1980).

2   Auditorium and proscenium boxes, Longacre Theatre, 1913

1   The exterior of the Longacre is a well-composed essay on 18th-century French classicism that exhibits architect Herts's devotion to design in the Beaux Arts tradition. Nevertheless, the Longacre lacked the panache and individuality of the New Amsterdam and Lyceum theatres, which Herts designed in partnership with Hugh Tallant. Unlike many theatres, the Longacre has a facade that is cleaner today than when it was opened; the large electric displays right and left are gone, replaced by a smaller, less garish sign centered on the entrance.

2   With its conventional two-balcony auditorium and modified frame proscenium, the Longacre made a handsome appearance. It was decorated with swag-and-fleuret plasterwork on the box and balcony fronts, and bronze lamps flanked the proscenium. The cornice held stylized comic masks that resembled medieval pith helmets. The crystal chandelier represented a departure for Herts: When working with Hugh Tallant, he honored his partner's belief that suspended lights were a distraction to both actors and audience.

Candler Theatre

226 West 42nd Street & 223-29 West 41st Street

Willauer, Shape & Bready, Architects (building) • Thomas White Lamb, Architect (theatre)

Opened (films) May 7, 1914; 1051 seats • Reopened (plays) as Cohan and Harris Theatre, October 25, 1916

Asa Candler, the principal owner of the Coca Cola Company, was also a shrewd real estate investor. In 1912 he built a 28-story skyscraper that was, for a brief time, the tallest structure on 42nd Street, and the next year he built a theatre on an adjoining lot. Although the auditorium was on 41st Street, its entrance, albeit narrow, was on 42nd Street. Candler leased his theatre to a partnership of George M. Cohan, Sam H. Harris, and George Kleine, a motion picture pioneer. At first the Candler was strictly a film house, but box office receipts were disappointing. Cohan and Harris then became the sole lessees and renamed the Candler for themselves, the Cohan and Harris Theatre. The house quickly became one of their most profitable operations. Among the hits were *Hitchy-Koo of 1917* and *The Royal Vagabond* (1919). After Cohan and Harris went their separate ways in 1920, Harris continued to manage the theatre. He booked John Barrymore's record-breaking run in *Hamlet* (1921), Owen Davis' Pulitzer Prize-winning *Icebound* (1923), and Cornelia Otis Skinner and Clark Silvernail in *White Collars* (1925). In 1926, Harris sold the theatre to the Shuberts, who subleased it to motion picture presenters in addition to booking a few plays. The Shuberts disposed of the house in 1933, as part of their bankruptcy settlement, and Asa Candler's proud old theatre became a grind film house.

2   Auditorium, toward proscenium, Candler Theatre, 1914

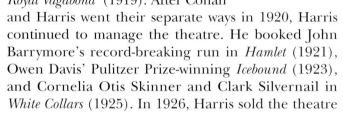

3   Auditorium, Candler Theatre, 1914

1   Harris became sole manager of the theatre in 1921 and renamed it for himself. In this 1934 photograph, the facade looks much the same, except for the name, as it did when it opened. The narrow theatre entrance is on the ground floor of the 28-story terra-cotta-clad Candler Building.

2   The Italian Renaissance decor of the Candler auditorium was dominated by the ornate plasterwork around the proscenium, which contrasted with the sparer treatment of the boxes. A wide, shallow saucer dome dominated the ceiling. In its outer rim were twelve hanging light fixtures.

3   The Candler had only one balcony, at the rear of which was the film projection booth. Murals by Albert Herter decorated the promenade at the back of the orchestra.

Punch & Judy Theatre

153-55 West 49th Street

Murphy & Dana, Architects • Opened November 10, 1914; 299 seats
Reopened as Charles Hopkins Theatre, 1926

◄ 1

2 Auditorium, Punch & Judy Theatre, 1914

Despite its name, the Punch & Judy was not built for puppet shows or other children's plays but for experimental modern works and revivals of lesser-known classics. This formula, devised by actor and sometime-producer Charles Hopkins, turned out to be a commercial flop. Few of Hopkins' early bookings achieved good runs. The best of the lot was *Rollo's Wild Oat* (1920), a comedy starring Roland Young. Hopkins' judgment (or luck) improved after he renamed the theatre for himself in 1926. Notable productions were *Devil in the Cheese* (1926), with Bela Lugosi, and

Frederic March in *Mrs. Moonlight* (1930), which ran for almost a year. In 1933 the Hopkins was leased to motion picture exhibitors. Renamed the World Theatre in 1935, it specialized in foreign films until its management turned to pornography in the 1960s. The old theatre's most famous presentation premiered in 1972—the pornographic classic *Deep Throat*, starring Marilyn Chambers. The theatre was torn down in 1987 to make way for an expansion of Rockefeller Center.

1 The smooth, unpretentious stucco facade of the Punch & Judy, huddled between two New York brownstones, was enlivened by color paintings of the battling puppets. In the early years a musician in medieval costume would appear on the roof and sound a trumpet fanfare that meant "Curtain going up!"

2 London's Blackfriars Theatre of Shakespearean fame was the inspiration for the Punch & Judy auditorium. The stage was small by Broadway standards, 39 feet wide and 31 feet deep. Resembling a chapel, the main floor held 247 seats, with the remainder in side and rear wall boxes. With its oak beams, rough plaster walls, and small seating capacity, the theatre's design represented the ideals of the nonprofit "little theatre" movement

Morosco Theatre

217-25 West 45th Street

Herbert J. Krapp, Architect • Opened February 5, 1917; 923 seats

◀ 1

In gratitude for California producer Oliver Morosco's help in breaking the Theatrical Syndicate's monopoly, the Shuberts agreed to finance and build a New York theatre for him. Morosco's tenure lasted only seven years, terminated by a messy divorce suit, but he achieved some commercial successes—Mary Roberts Rinehart's *The Bat* (1920) ran for 867 performances—and booked two winners of the Pulitzer Prize—Eugene O'Neill's *Beyond the Horizon* (1920) and George Kelly's *Craig's Wife* (1925). The Shuberts then took over. The 1920s and early '30s generated little excitement for the Morosco, although Thornton Wilder's *Our Town* (another Pulitzer winner) transferred from Henry Miller's Theatre in 1938 and Gertrude Lawrence starred in *Skylark* (1939). The next decade brought Noel Coward's *Blithe Spirit* (1941), John Van Druten's *The Voice of the Turtle* (1943), and Arthur Miller's classic, *Death of a Salesman* (1949; Pulitzer Prize). Two more Pulitzer winners at the Morosco were Tennessee Williams' *Cat on a Hot Tin Roof* (1955) and *The Shadow Box* (1977). In 1968 the Morosco, which had been part of the City Playhouses group since 1943, was sold to investors affiliated with Bankers Trust Company. The next thirteen years held several noteworthy productions, including the English trilogy *The Norman Conquests* (1976) and the long-running Hugh Leonard play, *Da* (1978). The Morosco and four neighboring theatres were demolished in 1982—after widespread protests centering particularly on the Helen Hayes (formerly Folies Bergere)—to clear the land for the Marriott Marquis Hotel.

2 Auditorium, Morosco Theatre, 1917

1 In this silhouette of the Morosco, the theatre appears all alone on West 45th Street, which was in fact a bustling theatrical thoroughfare. Architect Krapp enlivened what might have been an austere white brick facade by having the bricks laid in a Flemish bond pattern with regularly protruding headers. Classical terra-cotta detailing and a pressed metal cornice also add some distinction to the street front.

2 An airy and spacious auditorium, with graceful Adamesque detailing, was a welcome contrast to the cramped entryways at the Morosco. Almost twice as wide as it was long, the fan-shaped space had only one balcony. The auditorium had clear sight lines and excellent acoustics, making it a model of the ideal commercial theatre.

3 The Morosco had a small box office vestibule walled in veined white marble that led to a narrow, curving promenade that ran the width of the theatre.

◄ 3 Box office vestibule, Morosco Theatre, 1917

Broadhurst Theatre

235-43 West 44th Street

Herbert J. Krapp, Architect • Opened September 27, 1917; 1120 seats

2 Auditorium, Broadhurst Theatre, 1917

The Broadhurst and Plymouth theatres were built side by side, almost mirror images of each other. Hewn from the same stone, they rose on Shubert land left over from their Astor lease on which the Shubert and the Booth theatres had been built in 1913. Both Broadhurst and Plymouth were managed by others—playwright George Broadhurst of his eponymous house (of which he was co-lessee) and Arthur Hopkins, who was looking for a house larger than his floundering Punch & Judy. The architect referred to the Broadhurst as "the Greek theatre," in contrast to the "Renaissance" Plymouth, presumably referring to the interior decor. Indeed, the Broadhurst features Doric columns and other ancient Greek motifs. George Broadhurst opened his playhouse with G. B. Shaw's *Misalliance* (1917) and had great popular success with Henry Hull's *39 East* (1919). Other notable bookings were Michael Arlen's *The Green Hat* (1925), with Katharine

Cornell, and Lee Tracy in the long-running *Broadway* (1926). Under direct Shubert management from 1929, the Broadhurst was the venue for Sidney Kingsley's Pulitzer Prize-winning *Men in White* (1933), Humphrey Bogart in Robert E. Sherwood's *The Petrified Forest* (1934), and Helen Hayes as the unforgettable *Victoria Regina* (1935). Kingsley returned to the Broadhurst with *Detective Story* (TRF 1950), which was followed by a long-running revival of *Pal Joey* (1952). Other hit musicals at the Broadhurst were *Auntie Mame* (1956), the Pulitzer Prize-winning *Fiorello!* (1959), the original production of Kander and Ebb's *Cabaret* (1966), the first Broadway appearance of *Grease* (transferred from the Off-Broadway Eden Theatre in 1972), and Bob Fosse's *Dancin'* (1978). Peter Shaffer's *Amadeus* (1980) was one of the few dramas to play the Broadhurst during this period. Kander and Ebb returned in 1993 with *Kiss of the Spider Woman*.

1   The exterior of the Broadhurst is noteworthy for its sparing use of decoration. The architects used some stone and terra-cotta trim but relied mostly on variations in the pattern of the brickwork to set the theatre apart from its neighbors. The corner entrance has a broken-pediment enframement with an oval cartouche.

2   Classic Greek motifs are highlighted throughout the Broadhurst auditorium. It featured Doric columns above the proscenium boxes, a cornice of alternating triglyphs and medallions, stylized pediments over the exit doors, and friezes of horsemen on the box fronts and over the proscenium arch.

Plymouth Theatre

234-40 West 45th Street

Herbert J. Krapp, Architect • Opened October 10, 1917; 1036 seats

Arthur Hopkins had five years experience as a Broadway producer when the Shuberts chose him as manager of the Plymouth Theatre. He proved his mettle over the next thirty-odd years with such notable bookings as the brothers John and Lionel Barrymore in *The Jest* (1919), the Maxwell Anderson-Laurence Stallings war play *What Price Glory?* (1924), and Philip Barry's *Holiday* (1928). Pulitzer Prizes were won by Robert E. Sherwood's *Abe Lincoln in Illinois* (1938) and Thornton Wilder's *The Skin of Our Teeth* (1942). After Hopkins, the Shuberts took over management of the Plymouth, offering such successes as Maurice Evans in *Dial M for Murder* (1952), Henry Fonda and an all-star cast in *The Caine Mutiny Court-Martial* (1954), and Claudette Colbert and Charles Boyer in *The Marriage-Go-Round* (1958). The 1960s were dominated by three Neil Simon comedies—*The Odd Couple* (1965), *The Star-Spangled Girl* (1966), and *Plaza Suite* (1968). Peter Shaffer's *Equus* (1974) attracted three great leading men during its run—Anthony Hopkins, Anthony Perkins, and Richard Burton. More recent productions have included the Royal Shakespeare Company's *The Life and Adventures of Nicholas Nickleby* (1981), and Wendy Wasserstein's transfer from Off-Broadway, *The Heidi Chronicles* (1989).

2 Renovated auditorium, Plymouth Theatre, 1917

1 Like the Broadhurst, the Plymouth Theatre is built of buff brick with rounded corners and with little exterior decoration. The Plymouth also has some terra-cotta detailing that enframes the brick in panels. A narrow alley provides a link between the two houses, which are mirror images of each other.

2 The interior of the Plymouth is Adamesque, resembling other theatres built by Herbert J. Krapp for the Shuberts. The arch openings are segmental, rather than squared off as in the Broadhurst, and the sounding board over the proscenium further enframes the stage. Looking much the same today as when it was built, the Plymouth is still decorated with low-relief plasterwork, friezes of urns, wreaths, and other classical figures.

Henry Miller's Theatre

124-30 West 43rd Street

Ingalls & Hoffman and Paul R. Allen, Associated Architects • Opened April 1, 1918; 946 seats

2 Auditorium and proscenium, Henry Miller's Theatre, 1929

The English-born actor Henry Miller began to produce his own shows in 1906, leasing the Princess Theatre from the Shuberts. With the real estate firm of William A. White he built his own house, where he acted and produced into the 1920s. Among his notable plays at the theatre were *The Famous Mrs. Fair* (1919) and *Quarantine* (1924) with Helen Hayes. Henry's son Gilbert began managing the theatre in 1926, when he booked a hit, *The Play's the Thing*, by Ferenc Molnar, adapted by P. G. Wodehouse. Gilbert Miller bought the theatre in 1930 and became one of Broadway's most celebrated manager/producers. In

1934 *Personal Appearance* ran for over a year, and in 1936 Thornton Wilder's enduring *Our Town* won the Pulitzer Prize. T. S. Eliot's *The Cocktail Party* (1950), Agatha Christie's *Witness for the Prosecution* (1954), and *The Andersonville Trial* (1959) with George C. Scott were followed by *Under the Yum-Yum Tree* (1960) and *Enter Laughing* (1963) before the Miller, under new ownership, began to show pornographic films. The building also housed nightclubs, most famously the discotheque Xenon, and similar halls before returning to the ranks of Broadway theatres with a smash-hit, all-award-winning production of *Cabaret* in 1997.

1 Built of Flemish bond red brick and trimmed in white marble, the facade of Henry Miller's Theatre is neo-Georgian in style. Like the Little Theatre, the Miller is formally composed, with three central arched windows and pedimented end bays masking the side alleys and fire escapes. Overall, the theatre is domestic both in scale and character.

2 The Georgian detail of the auditorium is refined and simple, reinforcing the drawing room atmosphere for which both owner and architects were striving. Originally painted a light gray with amber brocade hangings, the Miller felt quite intimate for a 1000-seat house. Bucking the single-balcony trend, Henry Miller insisted on having a second balcony for theatregoers with modest budgets.

Selwyn Theatre

229-31 West 42nd Street & 240-48 West 43rd Street

George Keister, Architect • Opened October 3, 1918; 1051 seats

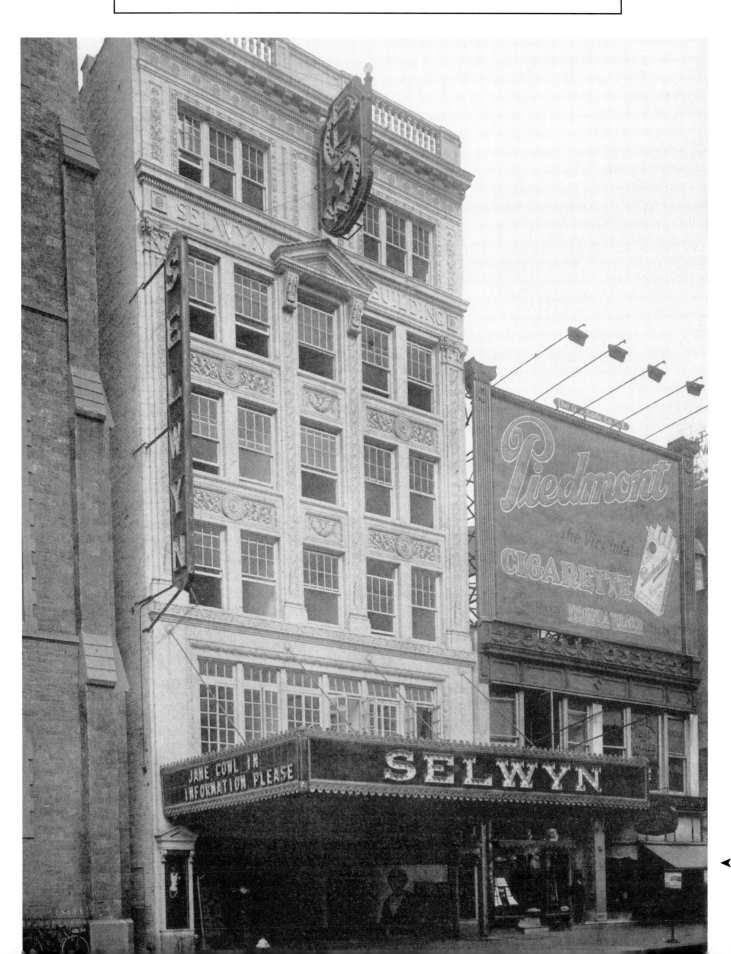

The Selwyn brothers from Cincinnati, Arch and Edgar, were well known on Broadway as actors, agents, producers, and, finally, landlords. They gained control of a large plot of land between 42nd and 43rd streets and announced plans for three new theatres. Their first was the Selwyn, built behind a six-story office tower, the Selwyn Building, just in time for the post-World-War-I theatrical boom. The redoubtable Jane Cowl opened the Selwyn with a flop, *Information Please*, but quickly redeemed herself with a respectable run in *The Crowded Hour*. The theatre's biggest hit opened after the Selwyn brothers split in 1927. *The Royal Family* (1927), written by George S. Kaufman and Edna Ferber, was a critically acclaimed satire on the Drew and Barrymore theatrical dynasties. After the Dietz & Schwartz revue *Three's a Crowd* (1931), with Fred Allen, Libby Holman, and Clifton Webb, the Selwyn presented eleven flops in a row before becoming a grind film house (under different ownership) in 1934. Experimental theatre briefly returned live drama to the Selwyn in 1950-51, when an-hour-long version of Sartre's *The Respectful Prostitute* was performed five times a day, between films, by several casts.

2 Auditorium, Selwyn Theatre, 1918

1 The Selwyn Building on West 42nd Street had a terra-cotta-trimmed facade and a rooftop balustrade. The entrance to the theatre, trimmed in the Italian Renaissance style, led to a long corridor and the auditorium, which was on 43rd street.

2 The shallow, single-balcony auditorium of the Selwyn Theatre illustrates the trend toward smaller-scaled playhouse design. The decor reflected an Italian influence with some Adamesque detailing. Frescos painted by Arthur Brounet over the boxes showed a dancer, jester, musician, and other performers in classical dress. Above, the saucer dome was cove-lit.

Times Square/Apollo Theatre

215-23 West 42nd Street • Eugene DeRosa, Architect

Opened September 30, 1920; 1057 seats • Opened November 18, 1920; 1194 seats

The Selwyn brothers completed their 42nd Street theatrical complex with these two theatres, which shared a common facade and sign. The west side of the marquee and vertical sign advertised the show at the Apollo, and the west side advertised the Times Square. The Apollo had its origin in the Bryant Theatre, built in 1910 as Times Square's first film-and-vaudeville house. When the Selwyns built the Times Square, they rebuilt the Bryant and renamed it for the Greek god of music and verse. In their brief tenures as legitimate theatres, the Times Square fared better than the Apollo. It opened with the popular Florence Reed in *The Mirage*, then languished until the breakup of the Selwyn partnership in 1925. Then the stage came to life with Anita Loos's *Gentlemen Prefer Blondes* (1926), Ben Hecht and Charles MacArthur's *Front Page* (1928), the innovative musical by Gershwin, Kaufman, and Ryskind, *Strike Up the Band* (1930), and Gertrude Lawrence and Laurence Olivier playing with Noel Coward in his *Private Lives* (1931). The Apollo got off to a slow start—the only bright spot was a tour-de-force for W. C. Fields, *Poppy* (1924)— but the Selwyns salvaged their finances with leases to exhibitors of silent films like *Stella Dallas* (1925-26). Producer George White subleased the Apollo beginning in 1926. His biggest successes were two editions of *George White's Scandals* (1926; 1931)

and *Flying High* (1931), with Bert Lahr and Kate Smith. The last Broadway show to offer songs by the great Vincent Youmans, *Take a Chance* (1932), was the Apollo's final hit. In the depths of the Depression, the Times Square, Apollo, and Selwyn theatres were forced into bankruptcy in 1933-34, and all three became grind film houses. The Apollo had a brief return to live theatre from 1979 to 1983. After extensive renovations, the New Apollo reopened with *On Golden Pond* (1979), followed by several productions, including a revival of Lanford Wilson's *Fifth of July* (1980). The theatre then returned to motion picture presentations and ended its days as the Academy, first

2   Auditorium, Times Square Theatre, 1920

1   The two-theatre limestone facade consisted of a seven-bay loggia with wrought iron screens and solid end bays with paned windows. The arrangement provided the Times Square auditorium with an impressive 42nd Street front and the Apollo with an entrance to its 43rd Street auditorium. The connecting corridor was richly paneled and pilastered in a variety of marbles.

2   The shallow, fan-shaped auditorium of the Times Square held slightly more seats in the balcony and four boxes than in the orchestra. The interior design was in the Empire style with some familiar Adamesque touches. A pair of half-dome plaster canopies over the boxes were draped in elegant black velvet.

a cabaret and then a venue for rock concerts. Before the house was demolished in 1996, some of its architectural elements were salvaged and subsequently integrated into the Ford Center for the Performing Arts. The 1821-seat Ford was built at a reported cost of $36 million on the land occupied by the Apollo and the old Lyric Theatre. Ford's entrance is on 43rd Street, through the elegantly restored Lyric front. As of 1999, the Times Square stands vacant amid the reconstruction of 42nd Street. Livent had offered to construct a restaurant and small theatre in the building but withdrew in the face of financial difficulties. Bidders for the space have included the World Wrestling Federation and others who would build retail or exhibit space but restore and maintain the old facade.

3   Auditorium and proscenium, Apollo Theatre, 1920

3   With a more traditionally Adamesque interior than the Times Square, the Apollo auditorium was also slightly larger. The original color scheme was venturesome—tan rose and peacock blue. Because of the fan-shaped configuration of the one-balcony house, no patron felt very far removed from the stage.

Ambassador Theatre

215-23 West 49th Street

Herbert J. Krapp, Architect • Opened February 11, 1921; 1193 seats

2 Auditorium and stage set for rehearsals, Ambassador Theatre, 1982

The Ambassador was the first theatre the Shuberts built on 49th Street, west of Broadway, which they planned to transform into a theatrical mecca to rival 42nd Street. The house did well in its first decade, not only with traditional Shubert operettas like Sigmund Romberg's *Blossom Time* (1921) and Victor Herbert's *Dream Girl* (1925), but also with dramas like Owen Davis' adaptation of *The Great Gatsby* (1926) and *The Last Mile* (1930), a prison story with Spencer Tracy. Revivals dominated the 1930s, along with some interesting productions like *The Straw Hat Revue* (1939), featuring newcomers Imogene Coca, Danny Kaye, Alfred Drake, and Jerome Robbins. After the Shuberts sold the building in 1935, the Ambassador was principally a motion picture house and broadcast studio until 1955, when the Shubert Organization reacquired it. In addition to serving as a transfer house for such hits as *The Diary of Anne Frank*, which arrived in 1957 after more than a year at the Cort, the Ambassador opened successes like *The Lion in Winter* (1966). Transfers like *Same Time, Next Year* (1978) and Bob Fosse's *Dancin'* (1980) and revivals like Arthur Miller's *A View From the Bridge* (1983) and *Ain't Misbehavin'* (1988) dominated more recent years. The outrageous *Bring in 'Da Noise, Bring in 'Da Funk* was a bright light in the 1990s.

1 Built of buff brick, the unpretentious facade of the Ambassador is noteworthy only for the architect's rounded east corner and manipulation of the patternwork, overlaying the bricks to create a false cornice and dividing the blank bay by blind arches.
(Photo on previous page)

2 In order to gain maximum usable space from the Shuberts' plot, the auditorium was sited diagonally, with the box office vestibule in the southeast corner and the stage in the northwest corner of the building. The balcony stairs were placed in the other corners, giving the auditorium the shape of an elongated hexagon.

3   Auditorum, house right, Ambassador Theatre, 1921

3   The rich interior of the Ambassador was restored by
the Shuberts and remains a feast of Adamesque fans,
cameos, and swags. A wide variety of surface contours
and a shallow, oval-shaped dome were used to enhance
the acoustics of the house.

Ritz Theatre

219-25 West 48th Street • Herbert J. Krapp, Architect

Opened March 21, 1921; 974 seats • Reopened as Walter Kerr Theatre, April 16, 1990

For most of its existence the Ritz was one of the few Broadway theatres never to have booked a hit or even a reasonably long-running play. Built in record time (sixty-six days) and on a tight budget for the ever-expanding Shuberts, the Ritz was initially leased to their onetime Theatrical Syndicate rival William B. Harris. He brought stars to the Ritz stage, including Ina Claire in *Bluebeard's Eighth Wife* (1921) and Alfred Lunt and Leslie Howard in *Outward Bound* (1924), but with little commercial success. After the Shuberts took over, they booked a number of interesting productions, including *Broken Dishes* (1929), Bette Davis's first significant role. *Alison's House* (1930), by Susan Glaspell (cofounder of the Provincetown Players), won the Pulitzer Prize but failed to give the Ritz much of a financial boost. It was abandoned during the Depression, then brought back to life (1937-1939) by the Federal Theatre Project. The Ritz was a broadcast studio from 1939 until 1969, except for a brief interlude with Leonard Sillman's *New Faces of 1943*, followed by *Tobacco Road*, transferred from the old Forrest Theatre. After a long fallow period, the Ritz was bought by Jujamcyn Theatres in 1983. Extensive renovations followed the purchase, and in 1990 the theatre was renamed for drama critic Walter Kerr. Since then, two of August Wilson's acclaimed plays, *The Piano Lesson* (1990; Pulitzer Prize) and *Two Trains Running* (1992), have run at the Walter Kerr, along with Tony Kushner's epic *Angels in America* (1993) and Terence McNally's *Love! Valor! Compassion!* (1996).

2   Auditorium, Ritz Theatre, 1921

1   The exterior of the Ritz can best be described as utilitarian in the extreme. Only some diamond-pattern brickwork and a bit of decorative railing on the fire escapes break up the plain wall.

2   The Ritz auditorium was Adamesque in design, relying upon raised plasterwork in a variety of patterned configurations for visual interest. Over the proscenium was a large lunette mural, artist unknown, depicting Diana the Huntress with two hounds. This work and two other murals, planned for the house but never installed, were restored as part of the 1980s renovation designed by Roger Morgan Studios.

National Theatre

208-16 West 41st Street • William Neil Smith, Architect

Opened September 1, 1921; 1164 seats • Reopened as Billy Rose Theatre, October 18, 1959

What had been an indoor tennis court on the edge of the theatre district was transformed by the Shuberts into a playhouse capable of handling both straight plays and small-scale musicals. Theatrical agent Walter Jordan was the theatre's titular landlord, but the Shuberts were in charge—and in 1927 they bought the building. Although it was somewhat removed from the red-hot theatrical center, after a modest beginning the National was able to attract a number of outstanding productions. Its first big hit was Vicki Baum's *Grand Hotel* (1930). Gertrude Lawrence and Noel Coward starred in a series of short plays by Coward, *Tonight at 8:30* (1936). Two critically acclaimed, commercially successful dramas were Lillian Hellman's *The Little Foxes* (1939) and Emlyn Williams' *The Corn Is Green* (1940). The Harold Rome musical revue *Call Me Mister* (1946) was followed by a number of familiar names: *Inherit the Wind* (1955), *Once More With Feeling* (1958), *The Wall* (1960), and *Who's Afraid of Virginia Woolf?* (1962). During this period the Shubert Organization was the subject of a U.S. antitrust investigation, which ultimately led to divestiture of several theatres, including the National. Showman Billy Rose bought the house, renovated it, and renamed it in honor of himself. In succeeding years a number of British imports came to the theatre—Peter Brook's production of *A Midsummer Night's Dream* (1971), Tom Stoppard's *Jumpers* (1974), Brian Davis' *Whose Life Is It Anyway?* (1979, and Harold Pinter's *Betrayal* (1980). The Nederlander family bought the theatre in 1978, renamed it the National and then the Nederlander in 1980. The house was leased to a church from 1987 until 1989. The hit musical from Off-Broadway, *Rent*, by Jonathan Larson, opened here in 1996 and has been running ever since.

2   Auditorium, Nederlander Theatre, 1983

1   Gray and grim, the National Theatre's nondescript facade fits right in with neighboring buildings on 41st Street, which has functioned as a back alley for glitzy 42nd Street for almost 100 years.

2   The National's red and gold, single-balcony auditorium had little of the traditional plaster decoration, although there were a few classical features around the proscenium. The renovation by Billy Rose did much to brighten up the old house but added nothing distinguished. Today's Nederlander, rundown and shabby, has proven to be a brilliant setting for the popular *Rent*, a musical about New York's new class of educated slum dwellers.

Jolson's 59th Street Theatre

926-32 Seventh Avenue and 205-207 West 58th Street • Herbert J. Krapp, Architect

Opened October 6, 1921; 1770 seats • Reopened as New Century Theatre, April 8, 1944

In the mid-19th century this site was occupied by a cafe, the Central Park Garden. Eventually, the building's size and proximity to the bridle paths of Central Park made it a natural for conversion to the Central Park Riding Academy. The last horses left in 1916, and the Shuberts decided to reconvert the building into a large theatre and name it for their popular star, Al Jolson. The opening production was Sigmund Romberg's long-forgotten *Bombo*, starring Al in blackface. The Jolson's biggest hit was another Romberg operetta, *The Student Prince in Heidelberg* (1924), the decade's longest-running musical. Artistically, the most important event was the twelve-week engagement of Constantin Stanislavski and his Moscow Art Theatre (1923). With Maria Ouspenskaya, Akim Tamiroff, and other actors, Stanislavski introduced his Method acting style to New York. Because of its location, a half-mile north of the central theatre district, Jolson's was one of the first theatres the Shuberts cast off in their 1931 bankruptcy. Over the succeeding thirteen years it was renamed seven times, offering films and varied live entertainment. The newly solvent Shuberts returned in 1944, refurbished Jolson's, and renamed it the New Century for their

2 Auditorium toward balcony, Jolson's 59th Street Theatre, 1921

old Century, which had been demolished in 1931. Hit followed hit in those buoyant years—*Up in Central Park* (1945), *High Button Shoes* (1947), *Inside U.S.A.* (1948), and Cole Porter's unforgettable *Kiss Me, Kate* (1948). As the postwar Broadway boom moderated and bookings at Times Square theatres became easier to get, producers were reluctant to bring their shows to this northern location. The Shuberts leased the theatre to NBC in 1953 and to a videotaping facility five years later. The building was demolished in 1962.

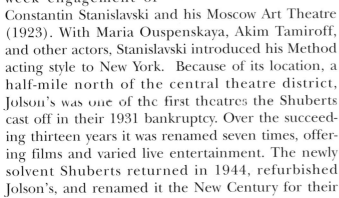

1 Only relatively minor changes were made to the facade of the old riding academy when it was converted to a theatre. The building's height was raised several stories to accommodate the Jolson's balcony, and large advertising signs were added to attract the public's attention.

2 The auditorium of Jolson's Theatre was long and narrow—the Shuberts wanted to save on reconstruction costs by keeping the walls of the original building. Orchestra boxes were along the side walls. Interior decoration was in the Shuberts' standard Adamesque style, with a few adornments to the ceiling and walls.

Music Box Theatre

239-47 West 45th Street

Charles Howard Crane, Architect; E. George Kiehler, Associate Architect • Opened February 22, 1921; 859 seats

One of Broadway's loveliest playhouses, the finely detailed Music Box Theatre has also proven to be one of its most successful. The intimate theatre was built by legendary songwriter Irving Berlin and his partner/producer, Sam H. Harris, as the home of Berlin's annual *Music Box Revues* (1921-24). Other musical attractions have included Cole Porter's first hit score, *Paris* (1928); the first musical to win a Pulitzer Prize, George and Ira Gershwin's *Of Thee I Sing* (1931), with book by George S. Kaufman and

Morrie Ryskind; and Irving Berlin and Moss Hart's topical revue *As Thousands Cheer* (1933). Other Depression-era hits were John Steinbeck's *Of Mice and Men* (1937) and Kaufman and Hart's enduring *The Man Who Came to Dinner* (1939). Sam Harris produced most of these hits. After he died in 1941, his share in the theatre passed to Berlin. Outstanding productions in the 1940s and '50s were John Van Druten's *I Remember Mama* (1944), Tennessee Williams' *Summer and Smoke* (1948), Terence

2   Auditorium, Music Box Theatre, 1921

1   The Regency-style limestone facade of the Music Box, like that of the Times Square/Apollo, consists of a double-height colonnaded loggia flanked by solid end bays, reminiscent of Philadelphia's Chestnut Street Theatre (1822), the famed "Old Drury." Delicately featured Palladian windows and paired pilasters add to the formal symmetry of the composition, while a homelike character is imparted by the mansard roof and shutters on the upper windows. Fire escapes are so well integrated into the design as to be virtually unnoticeable.

2   The interior of the theatre, decorated with Adamesque details and painted in ivory and soft green, was designed by architect C.H. Crane in collaboration with William Baumgarten. Lighting was originally provided by five-branch wall sconces and four crystal chandeliers. The sconces were replaced in the 1960s by simulated brass fixtures in what one critic called Miami Beach swank style, at odds with the original decor.

Rattigan's *Separate Tables* (1956), and three William Inge dramas—the Pulitzer Prize-winning *Picnic* (1953), *Bus Stop* (1955), and *The Dark at the Top of the Stairs* (1957). The longest runs at the Music Box have both been mysteries—Ira Levin's *Deathtrap* (1978) and Anthony Shaffer's *Sleuth* (1970). Other British imports at Berlin's playhouse included Harold Pinter's *The Homecoming* (1967), Alan Ayckbourn's *Absurd Person Singular* (1974), and the Royal Shakespeare Company's *Les Liaisons Dangereuses* (1987). The Music Box Theatre today is co-owned by the Berlin Estate and the Shubert Organization.

3 The archways over the boxes are flanked by attached columns and pilasters, and the metal box railings are finished in gilt. Pastoral murals decorate the half-domes over the boxes

3 Auditorium toward house right, Music Box Theatre, 1921

4 Downstairs lounge, Music Box Theatre, 1921

4 The clublike basement lounge, with mock fireplace, murals, and mirrors, is a pleasant surprise, given the neglect of these spaces in most Broadway houses.

Earl Carroll Theatre

753 Seventh Avenue & 160-66 West 50th Street

George Keister, Architect • Opened July 5, 1923; 998 seats • Reopened August 27, 1931; 3000 seats

◄ 1

Earl Carroll was a thirty-year-old songwriter-turned-producer when he convinced Texas oil millionaire William Edrington to back him in building a Broadway theatre. The new playhouse got off to a bad start with two flops, but then a musical produced by Lawrence Schwab, *The Gingham Girl* (1922), ran for eight months. The first edition of the *Earl Carroll Vanities* (1923) also proved to be profitable. Competitor Flo Ziegfeld booked the house for an Eddie Cantor show, *Kid Boots* (1923), but through the 1920s the Carroll was used principally for annual editions of the *Vanities* . (In 1925, however, Eugene O'Neill's masterful *Desire Under the Elms* moved here from the Off-Broadway Greenwich Village Theatre.) A clone of the *Vanities*, Earl Carroll's *Sketchbook* (1929), was the theatre's biggest hit. Carroll was riding high and began looking with envy at Ziegfeld's new playhouse on 55th Street and Roxy Rothafel's palatial new theatre just across 50th Street. He wanted a larger house where he could present films and live entertainment at prices low enough to attract a mass audience. In 1930 Carroll and Edrington bought the property adjacent to their theatre in order to build a showplace that would challenge Ziegfeld. They gave

2 Auditorium, French Casino theatre-restaurant, 1934

architect Keister and a brilliant scenic artist/interior designer, Joseph Babolnay, virtual carte blanche (and $4.5 million; a huge sum in that day of the nickel subway fare) to create a spectacular theatre. The 1931 edition of *Earl Carroll's Vanities* opened the new theatre to good reviews, but times had become hard.

1 The 1931 renovation of the Earl Carroll retained the Seventh Avenue office building and old-style facade but brought to the entrance on 50th Street a strikingly new look. The black-and-white zigzag lines, the cast aluminum fire escapes, and the streamlined marquees are all hallmarks of the Art Deco design popular at the time. *(Photo on previous page.)*

2 Most of the Earl Carroll's spectacular interior design was preserved when the building was transformed into a theatre-restaurant. Initially called the French Casino, it was renamed Casa Manana by Billy Rose when he took over in 1936.

3 Gold and magenta bands of varying widths ran across the ceiling of the auditorium to a central cove.

◄ 3   Ceiling detail, Earl Carroll Theatre, 1931

Box office receipts failed to cover Carroll's heavy expenses, and he lost the theatre. Sharpening the loss was Flo Ziegfeld's opening a revival of his hit *Show Boat* at the Carroll. Ever the entrepreneur, Earl set off for Hollywood, where the movie colony was prospering. Eventually, he was able to open a new Earl Carroll Theatre on Hollywood Boulevard in 1938 and regained his status as a top showman. Back in New York, the not-so-old Earl Carroll, after surviving the 1930s as a restaurant/nightclub, suffered conversion to retail space in 1940. In the process, one of New York's most dramatic Art Deco interiors was obliterated to make way for a five-and-ten-cent store. The building was demolished in 1990.

4 The spirit of the new Carroll's design is captured by the different shapes, lines, and colors around the proscenium arch. All lighting within the house was indirect, except for special effects that could bathe the stage and auditorium in a myriad of colors.

5 The spacious mezzanine lounge was made to seem even larger with the installation of a two-story-high mirror wall.

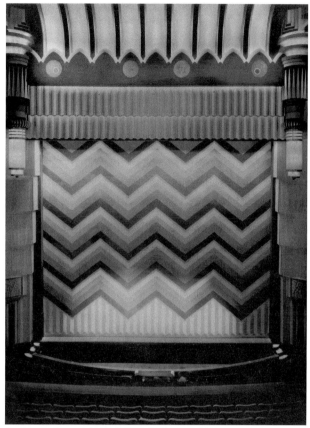

4   Proscenium arch, Earl Carroll Theatre, 1931

5   Mezzanine lounge, Earl Carroll Theatre, 1931

Imperial Theatre

249 West 45th Street and 238-50 West 46th Street

Herbert J. Krapp, Architect • Opened December 25, 1923; 1385 seats

As a replacement for the Shuberts' Lyric Theatre (only twenty years old but already considered out of date) the Imperial had much the same layout. A long corridor led from the narrow main entrance next door to the Music Box on bustling 45th Street to the Imperial auditorium on 46th Street, where land was less expensive because the crowds were much thinner. The new playhouse quickly became one of Broadway's most popular musical houses. Operettas dominated the early years. Rudolf Friml's biggest hit, *Rose-Marie* (1924), ran for over a year, and Sigmund Romberg's *The Desert Song* transferred from the Casino in 1927. Most of the great musical comedy names of the 1920s and '30s had their names on the Imperial marquee: the Gershwins, Rodgers & Hart, Dietz & Schwartz, Cole Porter. Mary Martin made her Broadway debut singing "My Heart Belongs to Daddy" in Porter's *Leave It to Me* (1938), then returned to the Imperial stage in the title role of *One Touch of Venus* (1943), by Kurt Weill, Ogden Nash, and S. J. Perelman. Irving Berlin was an Imperial favorite, with *Annie Get Your Gun* (1946) and *Call Me Madam* (1948), both starring Ethel Merman. Harold Rome's *Wish You Were Here* (1952) ran 598 performances, confounding the critics who had panned it, and Cole Porter's final Broadway show, *Silk Stockings*, opened in 1955. Frank Loesser's *The Most Happy Fella* followed in 1956. *Fiddler on the Roof* (1964) broke the record for long-running musicals with 3242 performances. Transfers also played a major role in enhancing the Imperial's reputation: Gypsy (TRF Broadway, 1960), *Cabaret* (TRF Broadhurst, 1967), and the astonishing *Les Miserables* (TRF Broadway, 1990), still running after over ten years.

2   Auditorium, Imperial Theatre, 1923

1   The Imperial facade on 45th Street, of white terra-cotta, and the wider front on 46th Street, of buff brick, cannot be said to be particularly distinguished. Only the theatre marquee and advertising signs give any indication that this is a place of amusement.

2   Inside, the Imperial is impressive. The long corridor from 45th Street, originally lined in white travertine, was recently redone in red-brown and gray marbles. Variations in the wall paneling of the auditorium and a low, slightly curved ceiling, impart surprising intimacy to so large a musical house. The shallow, fan-shaped seating in the orchestra also helps the theatre's acoustics.

Martin Beck Theatre

302-14 West 45th Street

G. Albert Lansburgh, Architect • Opened November 11, 1924; 1214 seats

After Martin Beck was ousted as general manager of the Orpheum Circuit, a vaudeville powerhouse in the West, from Chicago to California, he came back to Broadway. In 1915 he had been forced to give up his controlling interest in the Palace. Now he built a theatre of his own. Of the early productions he booked, only *The Shanghai Gesture* (1926) and *The Shannons of Broadway* (1927) were successful. Soon Beck leased his playhouse to the Theatre Guild, and shows like *The House of Connelly* (1931) and two Maxwell Anderson dramas, *Winterset* (1935) and *High Tor* (1937), played the Beck. Other notable productions of the 1930s included Aaron Copland's ballet *Billy the Kid* (1938) and the Douglas Moore-Stephen Vincent Benet opera *The Devil and Daniel Webster* (1938). Beck died in 1940, and the theatre continued under a series of managers. They booked a number of musical comedies, including *Cabin in the Sky* (1940), *On the Town* (TRF Adelphi, 1943), *Candide* (1956), *Bye Bye Birdie* (1960), and a popular transfer from Off-Broadway, *Man of La Mancha* (1968). Dramas included two anti-Nazi plays, *Watch on the Rhine* (1941) and *The Moon Is Down* (1942), Eugene O'Neill's *The Iceman Cometh* (1945), and two by Tennessee Williams, *The Rose Tattoo* (1948) and *Sweet Bird of Youth* (1959). Pulitzer Prize-winners *The Teahouse of the August Moon* (1953) by John Patrick and *A Delicate Balance* (1966) by Edward Albee also played the Beck, as did the Royal Shakespeare Company's *Marat/Sade* (1965). The Beck estate sold the theatre to Jujamcyn in 1968. Since then, many musicals have played the house, including *Into the Woods* (1985), Tommy Tune's *Grand Hotel* (1989), which moved to the larger Gershwin, and two hit revivals—*Guys and Dolls* (1992) and *The Sound of Music* (1998).

2   Auditorium toward house right, Martin Beck Theatre, c. 1930

1   With its unique design derived from the transitional Byzantine-Romanesque style of 12th-century northern Italy, the Beck stood in sharp contrast to many of the utilitarian houses built for the Shuberts in this same period. The building is not separated into an ornamented theatre front and a utilitarian stagehouse, but is treated as a single unit: a two-story arcade of cast-stone columns and rounded arches surmounted by two stories of offices faced in wine red brick.

2   The auditorium walls of the Martin Beck are of uneven, textured plaster. Clusters of Byzantine columns surround the proscenium, rising into fan vaults that form the sounding board. The boxfronts are treated as an undulating shallow S-curve and decorated with Byzantine motifs. Originally, tapestries hung on the side walls over the balcony, and a suspended circular wooden canopy covered in geometric designs by artist Albert Herter took the place of the usual saucer dome.

B.S. Moss' Colony Theatre

1681-85 Broadway & 226-40 West 53rd Street • Eugene DeRosa, Architect

Opened December 25, 1924; 1890 seats • Reopened as B.S. Moss' Broadway Theatre, December 8, 1930

◄ 1

The owner of a number of theatres in the New York City area, B.S. Moss built for himself a Broadway theatre with a stage large enough to accommodate not only films but also plays and other live entertainment. He opened with a silent film, *The Thief of Baghdad*, and for the next five years operated his Colony as a showcase for Universal Films. During the 1930s Moss booked a potpourri of film, vaudeville, and the occasional play. The Shuberts took over in 1939, changed the name on the marquee to Broadway, and switched to a bill that mixed short engagements of dance and theatre companies with popular-price transfers of musicals and new productions. In the latter category

2   Auditorium toward stage, Broadway Theatre, c. 1950

were Irving Berlin's *This Is the Army* (1942), Oscar Hammerstein's *Carmen Jones* (1943), Gian-Carlo Menotti's opera *The Saint of Bleecker Street* (1954; Pulitzer Prize), the Sammy Davis vehicle *Mr. Wonderful* (1956), and the enduring *Gypsy* (1959). The 1960s were not a good time for the Broadway. Over the years a series of insensitive alterations had obliterated much of its original elegance. Despite these problems, crowds came to see *Purlie* (1970), a sleeper hit. In 1974 the auditorium was reconfigured for Harold Prince's innovative production of Leonard Bernstein's *Candide*. The audience sat on stools and the musicians and performing areas were scattered throughout the house. British imports then took over, attracted by the theatre's large stage and seating capacity. Andrew Lloyd Webber's *Evita* (1979) ran for 1567 performances. Following major restoration by stage designer Oliver Smith, the theatre reopened with *Les Miserables* (1987), produced by Cameron Mackintosh. When Mackintosh was unable to find an open theatre large enough to accommodate his *Miss Saigon* (1991), with its spectacular helicopter landing, he arranged to move 'Les Miz' to the Imperial. Both plays are still running.

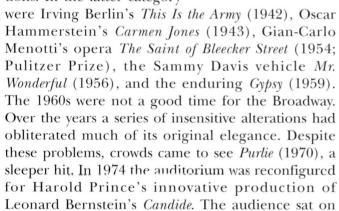

1   B.S. Moss' Colony was one of the great movie palaces of the silent film era, when "concert orchestras," as billboarded on the double-story electric sign, often accompanied first-run films in New York and other cities. The building's facade was brick trimmed with terra-cotta, executed in the Italian Renaissance style.

2   The auditorium of the Colony/Broadway is similar in layout and design to many of the mid-sized movie palaces designed in the office of Thomas Lamb, where architect Eugene DeRosa got his start. The decoration is Italian Renaissance in derivation, with many Adamesque elements. Marbles, bronzes, and gilt were used generously throughout the house.

3   Like the Palace, the Broadway became part of the overall design of a new skyscraper, in this case an office building that was cantilevered over the theatre's auditorium. The architectural firm of Fox & Fowle had the Broadway's facade resurfaced in polished granite.

◄ 3   Exterior, Broadway Theatre, 1991

Chanin's 46th Street Theatre

226-36 West 46th Street • Herbert J. Krapp, Architect

Opened February 7, 1925; 1429 seats • Reopened as Richard Rodgers Theatre, April 26, 1990

Real estate developers Irwin and Henry Chanin built six Times Square playhouses between 1924 and 1927; their 46th Street Theatre was the first. The Chanins were well financed and thus could afford to let their architect deviate somewhat from the Shuberts' "maximum seats at minimum cost" formula. Inevitably, however, the Shuberts became part of the deal. In need of another theatre to house their ever-growing portfolio of musicals, they leased the house from the outset. Among their hits were the long-running *Good News!* (1927) and *Follow Thru* (1929), both by the team of DeSylva, Brown, and Henderson. The Shuberts took ownership of the building in 1931, in a deal involving their Century on Central Park West. Olsen and Johnson's zany *Hellzapoppin* opened at the 46th

2   Auditorium toward house right, 46th Street Theatre, 1985

Street in 1938, followed by Cole Porter's *DuBarry Was a Lady* (1939) and *Panama Hattie* (1940). In 1945 the Shuberts sold the theatre to City Playhouses, an investment group. City booked some big hits, including Burton Lane and Yip Harburg's *Finian's Rainbow* (1947) and Abe Burrows and Frank Loesser's *Guys and Dolls* (1950). After Maxwell Anderson's chilling drama *The Bad Seed* (1954), Gwen Verdon held the stage with three big musicals—*Damn Yankees* (1955), *New Girl in Town* (1957), and *Redhead* (1959).

Burrows-Loesser's *How to Succeed in Business Without Really Trying* (1961) won the Pulitzer Prize in 1961. Another hit was Bob Fosse's production of Kander and Ebb's *Chicago* (1975). In 1982 the Nederlander organization bought the house and succeeded with some straight plays—notably August Wilson's Pulitzer-Prize-winning *Fences* (1987) and two Neil Simon comedies, *Lost in Yonkers* (1991) and *Laughter on the 23rd Floor* (1993). The 46th Street was renamed in honor of composer Richard Rodgers in 1990.

1   The facade of the 46th Street Theatre is more elaborate than all the work Krapp had done for the Shuberts. The white brick wall is embellished with a handsome cornice and balustrade, a rusticated sidewalk front, and sculptured panels of classical theatrical masks. A decorative triple-arched loggia between Corinthian columns also served as a screen for the balcony fire escape. The trim is terra-cotta. Adjacent is a seven-story stagehouse and dressing room wing faced in utilitarian buff brick.

2   The 46th street was the first Broadway house to employ the so-called stadium seating plan, with the orchestra rising at a relatively steep pitch all the way to the back of the house. The lobby is underneath the rear orchestra. Some sight lines in the house are not ideal because the balcony overhang reduced the stage picture for some patrons in the rear orchestra.

3   Adamesque plasterwork was used to enhance the overall look of the auditorium, with shell moldings forming arches on the walls. The boxes are decorated with wave friezes.

◄ 3   Proscenium boxes, Chanin's 46th Street Theatre, 1925

Guild Theatre

243-59 West 52nd Street • Crane & Franzheim, Architects

Opened April 13, 1925; 914 seats • Reopened as Virginia Theatre, June 27, 1982

The Theatre Guild was founded in 1919 and rapidly became one of the most respected institutions on Broadway. After three successful seasons at the Garrick, the Guild attracted enough money and support to have a building of its own, with an up-to-date theatre and space for an acting school and offices and other amenities. The opening production was G. B. Shaw's *Caesar and Cleopatra*, starring Helen Hayes and Lionel Atwill. Alfred Lunt and Lynn Fontanne were early supporters of the Guild and appeared at the theatre in *Caprice* (1928) and *The Taming of the Shrew* (1935). This period also saw the production of two plays by Eugene O'Neill, *Mourning Becomes Electra* (1931) and *Ah, Wilderness!* (1933). A string of failures beginning in 1937 decimated the Guild's treasury and forced it to lease the theatre to WOR Mutual Radio in 1943. The Guild Theatre was sold to the American National Theatre and Academy in 1950 and renamed ANTA Playhouse. At this time the house was also remodeled into a severely functional space devoid of all decoration. After being leased to the American Academy of Dramatic Arts in 1953-54, the theatre became a combination

2   Auditorium, house left, Guild Theatre, 1925

house, housing ANTA works as well as plays by independent producers. Among notable shows during this period were a musical, *Say, Darling* (1958); two Pulitzer-Prize-winning dramas, *J.B.* (1958) and *No Place to Be Somebody* (1964); British imports *A Man for All Seasons* (1961) and *The Royal Hunt of the Sun* (1965); and a revue, *Bubbling Brown Sugar* (1976). The ANTA

organization was merged into the Kennedy Center, and its New York theatre was sold to a new commercial managing group, Jujamcyn. They renamed the theatre Virginia for one of their partners, Virginia Binger, and booked a number of musicals, including *City of Angels* (1989) and *Jelly's Last Jam* (1992).

1   The design for the facade of the Guild was based on the grand villas of 15th-century Tuscany. Faced in stucco with stone quoin trimwork, the domestic aspect of the building was enhanced by its tile roof overhang, shutters on the windows, and the triple-arch loggia above the main entrance.

2   All public spaces within the Guild followed the Mediterranean design of the exterior. Walls were finished in rough plaster with open arched entryways and tapestries flanked by a pair of Baroque cartouches on the side walls. Although the proscenium was not flanked by boxes or ornate plaster filigree work, it nevertheless dominated the room through the striking contrast of its rich brocade drape with the bare plaster walls.

Forrest Theatre

230-38 West 48th Street • Herbert J. Krapp, Architect

Opened November 24, 1925; 1075 seats • Reopened as Eugene O'Neill Theatre, November 19, 1959

In 1921 the Shubert brothers planned to build six theatres on 48th and 49th streets west of Broadway. They opened three very quickly, then waited until 1925 to work out a deal for a Shubert-managed theatre in a hotel-and-theatre complex to be built by investors. Both theatre and hotel were named Forrest in honor of Edwin Forrest, the great nineteenth-century American tragedian. In its early days, the theatre offered few bright attractions. Only *On the Spot* (1930) with Anna May Wong and *As Husbands Go* (1930) managed to run more than 100 performances. The Shuberts disposed of their interest in the Forrest as part of the 1934 bankruptcy settlement, only to see *Tobacco Road* transfer from the Booth in 1935 and run for the next six years. The theatre was renamed Coronet in 1945

2   Auditorium, house left, Forrest Theatre, 1925

and housed Elmer Rice's *Dream Girl* (1945) and Arthur Miller's first Broadway success, *All My Sons* (1947). Producer Lester Osterman bought the theatre in 1953; among his notable presentations were the Arthur Miller double bill *A View from the Bridge* and *A Memory of Two Mondays* (1955) and Jean Anouil's *The Waltz of the Toreadors* (1959). The house was renamed for Eugene O'Neill in 1959. Neil Simon and producer David Cogan bought the theatre in 1967 and oversaw an extensive remodeling, inside and out. Not surprisingly, they then booked a string of comedies written by Simon, including *The Prisoner of Second Avenue* (1971) and *California Suite.* Jujamcyn took over the playhouse in 1982 and had long runs with the musicals *Big River* (1985) and *Grease* (1994; revival).

1   The original facade of the Forrest Theatre, as shown in somewhat idealized form in Herbert Krapp's drawing, was of brick and terra-cotta and featured a single-story wrought iron balcony over the theatre entrance. The hotel was a typical commercial building of the time. In later renovations the theatre was faced in gray stucco, the balcony was redesigned and doubled in height

2   Motifs reminiscent of ancient Rome decorate the low-relief plasterwork. Some Spanish influence is also evident, most notably in the triptych arches of the box openings within a larger blind arch..

3   Inside the theatre, many repaintings have obliterated the original red and gold decor. Most of the fixtures, including the chandeliers and ornamental railings, are still in place. The original Adamesque decoration continues to delight theatregoers.

3   Auditorium and stage, Eugene O'Neill Theatre, 1987

Biltmore Theatre

261-65 West 47th Street

Herbert J. Krapp, Architect • Opened December 7, 1925; 903 seats

The boom in Times Square construction reached West 47th Street in the late 1920s, as four major structures—all by architect Herbert J. Krapp—were built: the Biltmore, Mansfield, and Ethel Barrymore theatres, and the Hotel Edison. The Biltmore was the second theatre built by the Chanin brothers in their attempt to become a real estate powerhouse on Broadway. It's a smallish house, intended for drama and light comedy. Opening with a transfer from George M. Cohan's Theatre, *Easy Come, Easy Go,* starring Victor Moore, the new Biltmore also offered Sergei Eisenstein's classic *The Battleship Potemkin* (1926) and *The Barker* (1927), with Walter Huston and Claudette Colbert. In the Depression, the Chanins lost control of the theatre, which was briefly home to the Federal Theatre's Living Newspaper Project. Then Warner Brothers bought the building to house George Abbott productions like *Brother Rat* (1936), a military school musical farce, and *What a Life!* (1938). Non-Abbott hits included *My Sister Eileen* (1940), *The Heiress* (1947), and David Merrick's first Broadway production, *Clutterbuck* (1949). The Biltmore was converted to a CBS television studio in 1952. David Cogan bought the house in 1958 and three years later reopened it to live shows. Elizabeth Ashley starred with Art Carney in *Take Her, She's Mine* (1961) and with Robert Redford in *Barefoot in the Park* (1963). The Off-Broadway "love-rock musical" *Hair,* redesigned by Tom O'Horgan, ran at the Biltmore for over four years, beginning in April 1968. But the theatre's location, just off the Eighth Avenue "strip," failed to attract strong tenants, and David Cogan sold it in 1986. The interior was declared a New York City landmark in 1987, but the house remained dark, falling prey to looters and squatters. Although the Nederlanders in association with producer Stewart Lane bought the building in 1993, its future remains uncertain.

2   Auditorium, house right, Biltmore Theatre, 1925

1   The Biltmore facade is of white brick and terra-cotta. Corinthian pilasters and elaborate cornices are the principal design elements, with neo-Classic rustication at ground level. The fact that the fire escapes are on the sides, and the signage was comparatively discreet, made the now-shabby Biltmore one of the most attractive buildings in the theatre district.

2   To maximize seating capacity, the Biltmore auditorium was designed to run at a slight angle back from the street. At orchestra level the auditorium seating was in a horseshoe shape. The side walls were divided into panels by paired pilasters, and the ceiling was dominated by a shallow dome and chandelier. The Adamesque detailing was most elaborate around the proscenium; on the sides, the usual boxes were replaced by a pair of blind arches with faux box entries.

Mansfield Theatre

256-62 West 47th Street • Herbert J. Krapp, Architect

Opened February 15, 1926; 1075 seats • Reopened as Brooks Atkinson Theatre, September 12, 1960

2 Auditorium toward proscenium, Brooks Atkinson Theatre, 1985

The Chanin brothers named their third Times Square playhouse for the great American actor Richard Mansfield. The theatre got off to a slow opening, although *The Ladder* (1926), a play about reincarnation and starring Antoinette Perry, had a respectable run. The producer Lew Fields subleased the theatre and brought in two good shows— Rodgers and Hart's *Present Arms* (1928) and Herbert and Dorothy Fields' *Hello, Daddy* (1929)—and a true hit, Marc Connelly's Pulitzer-Prize-winning *The Green Pastures* (1930). After the cash-strapped Chanins lost their theatres in 1933, the Mansfield languished in failure and mediocrity. One bright spot was the transfer from a small theatre in Harlem of *Anna Lucasta* (1944), a drama of African-American family life in a small industrial town. Producer/investor

Michael Myerberg bought the house in 1945, then leased it to CBS Television in 1950. The theatre was returned to live performances in 1960, when it was renamed in honor of Brooks Atkinson, long-time drama critic of *The New York Times*. Neil Simon's first Broadway play, *Come Blow Your Horn* (1961), opened here, as did Rolf Hochhuth's controversial *The Deputy* (1964). The Nederlanders became co-owners of the Atkinson in 1967, buying the remainder after Michael Myerberg's death in 1974. The long-running *Same Time, Next Year* opened in 1975, and Lanford Wilson's *Tally's Folly* won the 1980 Pulitzer Prize. Outstanding British imports have played the Atkinson, among them *The Dresser* (1981), Michael Frayn's *Noises Off* (1985), and *Shadowlands* (1991).

1 Spanish motifs are readily evident in the facade of the Mansfield/Atkinson: the red tile roof, the spiral columns in the three Palladian archways, and the terra-cotta surrounds and modillions. Other elements, such as the rusticated street level appointments, are neo-Classic in derivation, though they are used here to enhance a romantic effect rather than the formal presentation of the nearby Biltmore and 46th Street theatres.

2 Although the theatre's interior has some elements of the Adamesque style popular at the time, the main design influence echoes the exterior in being modern Spanish. The interlocking Gothic arch plasterwork on the ceiling, heraldic shields, and the cast bronze chandeliers (now removed) were the dominant features. Above the box areas are murals depicting figures from the commedia dell-arte.

Ziegfeld Theatre

1341-47 Sixth Avenue & 101-7 West 54th Street

Joseph Urban and Thomas Lamb, Architects • Opened January 2, 1927; 1660 seats

Thomas Lamb's original plans for the Ziegfeld, in his standard neo-Georgian style, were rejected by both Flo Ziegfeld and his backer, William Randolph Hearst. They kept Lamb as associate but turned the job over to Joseph Urban, Flo's long-time design associate. Urban had been a successful architect in Vienna and since 1914 had worked in New York as a stage designer and director. The building he produced was hailed as a masterpiece. The first shows Ziegfeld brought into the theatre were also hits. In December 1927, after a successful run, *Rio Rita* was transferred into the Lyric to make room for an American classic, *Show Boat*. Joseph Urban was the principal designer for this enduring Kern-Hammerstein show. After *Show Boat*, however, the Ziegfeld Theatre went into precipitous decline. Even Fred and Adele Astaire and Marilyn Miller couldn't help save Vincent Youmans' *Smiles* (1930) from failure. After *The Ziegfeld Follies of 1931* ran for four months, a financially strapped Hearst leased the theatre to Loew's for use as a movie house.

2   Auditorium, Ziegfeld Theatre, 1927

In 1943, Billy Rose, who saw himself as successor to Ziegfeld, bought the theatre. He spruced up the house and reopened with a lavish revue, *Seven Lively Arts* (1944), with music and lyrics by Cole Porter. The show failed, and Rose soon reverted to the role of landlord. The theatre perked up with two revivals, *The Red Mill* (1945) and *Show Boat* (1946), and three outstanding original productions—*Brigadoon* (1947), *Gentlemen Prefer Blondes* (1949), and *Kismet* (1953). From 1955 to 1963 Rose leased his theatre to NBC Television. The theatre then returned to live productions for two years but failed to strike gold. The Rose estate sold the property to developers, and in 1966 the Ziegfeld was demolished despite outcries from preservationists outraged by the razing of Pennsylvania Station in 1963-64. Burlington House, an office tower, was built on the site, just to the east of a new movie theatre built by Loew's and named Ziegfeld.

1   The limestone-clad exterior of the Ziegfeld Theatre was described by its architect, Joseph Urban, as a mammoth poster for the musical shows on its stage. Stylistically, the facade combined elements of the Viennese Secession movement with sculptural symbolism of a theatrical cast. The bowed front suggested the curve of the auditorium within, while the central facade was a representation of a stylized proscenium arch.

2   The Ziegfeld auditorium was an egg-shaped ellipse with the proscenium at its narrow end; the balcony line was a wide, shallow curve. The unorthodox shape was pleasing to the eye but not to the ear; it was thought to be the cause of acoustic problems that bedeviled the house for years. The walls and ceiling were covered by a huge mural, "The Joy of Life," by Lillian Gaertner. The work was a stylized representation of a medieval tapestry depicting figures hunting, dancing, and courting amid fields of foliage and flowers.

3   The grand lounge on the mezzanine level combined traditional furnishings with an undulating wall surface and a canopy-like ceiling decorated by artist Willy Pogany.

◄ **3**   Mezzanine lounge, Ziegfeld Theatre, 1927

Royale Theatre

242-50 West 45th Street

Herbert J. Krapp, Architect • Opened January 11, 1927; 1172 seats

The Royale Theatre and the Theatre Masque, on 45th Street, and the Golden Theatre, on 44th Street, were built by the Chanins as part of the Lincoln Hotel (renamed Milford Plaza; 1981) complex that fronted on Eighth Avenue. The Royale was intended primarily as a venue for musical comedies but had little initial success with this formula. From 1927 until 1930, when the house was run by the Chanin organization, and from 1930 until 1934, when it was managed by the Shuberts, only three of the shows that opened at the Royale made back their investments—Mae West's *Diamond Lil* (1928), *Stepping Sisters* (1930; TRF Waldorf), and *When Ladies Meet* (1932). Maxwell Anderson's drama *Both Your Houses* (1934) ran only four weeks but won the Pulitzer Prize. Then the house was either dark or on lease to CBS Radio until 1941, when the first truly outstanding production to play on its stage, *The Corn Is Green*, transferred from the Broadhurst. Other successful shows followed: Mae West's *Catherine Was Great* (1944), *The Magnificent Yankee* (1946), *Medea* (1947), Leonard Sillman's *New Faces of 1952*, and *The Boy Friend* (1954). Frank Gilroy's *The Subject Was Roses* won the 1964 Pulitzer Prize. The mega-hit *Grease* transferred from the Off-Broadway Eden via the Broadhurst to the Royale in 1972 and remained until 1980, breaking the Broadway record for long runs. Another

2 Royale Theatre and Theatre Masque, architect's drawing of facade, 1926

transfer from Off-Broadway, *Joseph and the Amazing Technicolor Dreamcoat*, ran at the Royale from 1982 until 1983. In the late 1980s Tony Awards were showered on players at the Royale: Judd Hirsch in *I'm Not Rapaport* (1986), Bernadette Peters in *Song & Dance* (1986), Ron Silver in *Speed-the-Plow* (1988), and Philip Bosco in *Lend Me a Tenor* (1989). Hirsch was a repeat winner in *Conversations With My Father* (1992).

1   The Royale Theatre was built of variegated brick with terra-cotta detailing in the Spanish Renaissance manner. A five-arch window arcade masks the fire escape.

2   Built at the same time, the Royale and the Theatre Masque share a single facade with separate entrances. A pergola on the Royale's stagehouse, at left, matches a similar structure atop the Masque.

3   The auditorium of the Royale features the same mixture of Adamesque and Spanish-inspired detailing seen in the architect's earlier Mansfield, though here the ceiling is treated as an intersecting groin vault. The side wall arches hold colorful murals by Willy Pogany, entitled "Lovers of Spain." The original box drapes and proscenium valance featured stylized satin swans in flight.

◄ 3   Auditorium toward house left, Royale Theatre, 1927

Theatre Masque

252-56 West 45th Street • Herbert J. Krapp, Architect

Opened February 24, 1927; 799 seats • Reopened as John Golden Theatre, February 2, 1937

3 Proscenium from balcony, Theatre Masque, 1927

Like the Royale, the Theatre Masque did not fare well in its early days. Of the few successes, only *Goodbye, Again* (1932) played its full run at the house. Seating capacity was a problem. The record-setting *Tobacco Road* opened here in 1933 but the great demand for tickets made it prudent to move the show to a larger house, the Forrest, where it ran until 1941. John Golden, who became manager in 1937 and renamed the theatre for himself, booked the longest run, *Angel Street* (1941-44). In 1946 he subleased the theatre to an exhibitor of foreign films, but in 1950 the Shuberts took over and brought back legitimate theatre. Most successful at the Golden during the next two decades were comic revues—*A Party with Betty Comden and Adolph Green* (1958), Victor Borge's *Comedy in Music* (1953), Flanders & Swann's *At the Drop of a Hat* (1959), *An Evening With Mike Nichols and Elaine May* (1960), and *Beyond the Fringe* (1962). The late 1970s and early '80s saw a number of distinguished dramas, four of which won the Pulitzer Prize: *The Gin Game* (1977), *Crimes of the Heart* (1981), *'night Mother* (1983), and *Glengarry Glen Ross* (1984). William Finn's *Falsettos* opened here in 1992.

1 The facade of the Theatre Masque, like that of the adjoining Royale, was part of a single wall constructed of variegated brick with terra-cotta detailing in the Spanish Renaissance manner. The smaller Masque facade is a symmetrical composition centered on three blind arches.

2 Theatre Masque's interior had a strong Spanish flavor. With its rough plaster walls, wrought iron fixtures, and beam and corbel ceiling, it was the best example on Broadway of the Mission Revival style popular on the West Coast during the 1920s. The Gothic-arched doorways and vibrant fresco work on the beams and ceiling arches gave the space a medieval look. Though much of this work has been painted over, the theatre remains attractive.

Majestic Theatre

245-57 West 44th Street

Herbert J. Krapp, Architect • Opened March 28, 1927; 1762 seats

2 Auditorium toward house left, Majestic Theatre, 1927

The Majestic was built as a large house, about the same size as another Shubert theatre, Jolson's, but with superior ambiance and acoustics. Stadium-style seating in the orchestra and the steep balcony made for a large open space above most of the audience, but the theatre preserves an intimate feeling with its side wall arches extending well into the coved ceiling. The Majestic's early decades were filled with transfers from other Shubert theatres, and many of its seats were sold at discount prices. Second-hand hits included *Rio Rita* (1928), *On Your Toes* (1936), *Hellzapoppin* (1941), and *Junior Miss* (1943). In the postwar years a long line of hit musicals opened at the Majestic, beginning with Rodgers & Hammerstein's *Carousel* (1945) and continuing with the team's *Allegro* (1947), the Pulitzer-Prize-winning *South Pacific* (1949), *Fanny* (1954), *The Music Man* (1957), and *Camelot* (1960). The theatre returned to its role as a transfer house in the mid-1960s, with a varied bill that included *Funny Girl* (1966) as well as *42nd Street* (1981). The latter had left the Winter Garden to make way for *Cats* and proceeded to fill the Majestic's seats for the next six years. *The Phantom of the Opera* (1987) then moved into the Majestic, where it is still running (as is *Cats*, at the Winter Garden).

1 The facade of the Majestic is more massive in appearance than the Royale-Masque front. The building runs a uniform six stories, with decoration confined to a stylized Palladian motif over the entrance and a pair of wrought iron fire escape balconies. A Spanish Renaissance-style pediment identical to that on the Royale is centered on the theatre's roofline. At sidewalk level the decoration is rusticated terra-cotta.

2 The Shuberts' favored Adamesque detailing is broadly evident in the Majestic auditorium, though often enlarged in scale to keep up with the size of the house. The boxes are step-staggered along the side walls, uniting the balcony with the proscenium. The fan-shaped design gives the appearance of strong width, though in fact the auditorium is narrower than the average theatre of its size. The box office and lounge areas are beneath the rear of the orchestra.

3 A good source of profits for the Shuberts over the years, the Majestic has been subject to periodic renovations to maintain its elegant, theatrical flair. The auditorium looks much as it did in the 1920s, except for the installation of equipment to keep up with contemporary sound and lighting needs.

3 Auditorium toward proscenium, Majestic Theatre, 1985

Erlanger's Theatre

246-56 West 44th Street • Warren & Wetmore, Architects

Opened September 26, 1927; 1509 seats • Reopened as St. James Theatre, December 7, 1952; 1618 seats

A. L. Erlanger was one of the major powers in the Theatrical Syndicate, the Shuberts' arch-rival. Even so, he recognized that the theatrical center of 1920s New York was Shubert Alley. Thus he engaged the architects of the famed Grand Central Station to build his new playhouse in the heart of Shubert country, on 44th Street. The move was a flop. Erlanger had a decent run with only one

2 Auditorium from stage, Erlanger's Theatre, 1927

musical, *Fine and Dandy* (1930), before his finances collapsed and he lost the theatre. Lodewick Vroom then became the manager and renamed the theatre for a well-known London playhouse, the St. James. He booked Sigmund Romberg's *May Wine* (1935) and several other middling shows before the Shuberts leased the theatre in 1941. The St. James came alive in 1943 when Rodgers and Hammerstein's fabulous *Oklahoma!* began its record-breaking run (2212 performances). The Shuberts booked several other great musicals—including Frank Loesser's *Where's Charley?* (1948), R&H's *The*

King and I (1951), and *The Pajama Game* (1954)—before giving up the theatre as part of their antitrust settlement. Jujamcyn took over and, after an interior renovation, reopened the house with another Rodgers & Hammerstein musical, *Flower Drum Song* (1958). *Hello Dolly!* (1964) ran 2844 performances, breaking the house record set by *Oklahoma!*. Other hits have included *Barnum* (1980), *My One and Only* (1983), and *The Secret Garden* (1990). Two outstanding revivals, *Gypsy* (1989) with Tyne Daley and *A Funny Thing Happened on the Way to the Forum* (1996) with Nathan Lane, have also played the St. James.

1 The facade of Erlanger's Theatre is austere to the point of dullness, with its plain gray stucco front relieved only by some Georgian-style cast stonework and an elaborate double-height loggia made of wrought iron just above ground level. Abe Erlanger's offices atop the theatre were later taken over by another theatrical powerhouse, producer David Merrick.

2 Erlanger's Theatre was designed with a second balcony, a rarity in theatres built after 1920. The elaborate plaster-work often favored by the Shuberts was absent, as the theatre's upper walls were covered with frescos of Arcadian scenes.

3 One of the few elegant touches in the theatre, the drapery canopies over the proscenium boxes were removed in one of the renovations.

3 Auditorium toward proscenium, Erlanger's Theatre, 1927

Alvin Theatre

244-54 West 52nd Street • Herbert J. Krapp, Architect

Opened November 22, 1927; 1362 seats • Reopened as Neil Simon Theatre, June 29, 1983

Alvin is an amalgam of the names of the producers for whom it was named—ALex Aarons and VINton Freedley—by its builder, real estate mogul Alexander Pincus. From the beginning the Alvin was primarily a musical comedy house, opening with the Gershwins' *Funny Face*. Ethel Merman made her Broadway debut here in another Gershwin show, *Girl Crazy* (1930). Even the Depression failed to dim the Alvin's star. Cole Porter's *Anything Goes* (1934) was a hit, and the Gershwins' *Porgy and Bess* (1935), written with DuBose Heyward, was an artistic triumph. Other great musicals included Rodgers & Hart's *The Boys From Syracuse* (1938) and the Moss Hart-Kurt Weill-Ira Gershwin show, *Lady in the Dark* (1941). One of the few straight plays to open at the Alvin, Robert E. Sherwood's *There Shall Be No Night* (1940), won the Pulitzer Prize. More dramas followed the sale of the Alvin to producer Herman Bernstein in 1946. Two war memoirs, *Mister Roberts* (1948) and *No Time for Sergeants* (1955), were among the hits, as were two Stephen Sondheim musicals, *A Funny Thing Happened on the Way to the Forum* (1962) and *Company* (1970). *The Great White Hope* (1968) won the Pulitzer Prize, and *Annie* (1977)

2   Auditorium toward house right, Alvin Theatre, c. 1940

became the longest-running show at the theatre, with 2377 performances. The Nederlanders bought the building in 1977 and renamed it in 1984 for Neil Simon, whose hits *Brighton Beach Memoirs* (1983) and *Biloxi Blues* (1985) both played at the theatre.

3   Auditorium toward stage, Neil Simon Theatre, 1987

1   The red brick Georgian facade of the Alvin/Simon is dominated by three double-height arched windows with flanking side bays defined by white terra-cotta pilasters and false pediments. This architectural treatment is carried over to the stage and dressing room—a rarity for a Broadway theatre.

2   The auditorium is wide and deep, almost square in shape, with a single large balcony. The Adamesque plaster decoration was originally painted in pastel blue, gray, and lavender with gilt trim but has been repainted many times in white, thus obscuring some of the detail and destroying the original visual variety.

3   Stage lights dominate the theatre and what is left of its original decor in this 1987 view.

Hammerstein's Theatre

1697-99 Broadway and 213-23 West 53rd Street • Herbert J. Krapp, Architect
Opened November 30, 1927; 1204 seats • Reopened as Manhattan Theatre, September 8, 1931

Eight years after Oscar Hammerstein's death, his son Arthur, then at the zenith of his own career as a producer, built this theatre as a memorial to his father. (The foyer was dominated by a life-size bronze statue, discarded long ago, of the flamboyant Oscar in top hat and opera cape.) Arthur Hammerstein was a more sensible businessman than his father, but even he was caught in the Crash and forced into bankruptcy in 1931.During Hammerstein's tenure the only shows that managed to run more than 200 performances were *Good Boy* (1928) and *Sweet Adeline* (1929), both cowritten by Oscar Hammerstein II, Arthur's talented nephew. The theatre then had a series of managers. After the producing team of Schwab and Mandel failed, Billy Rose took over in 1934 and converted the house into a nightclub. Two years later the WPA Theatre Project leased the theatre for a short-lived production of T.S. Eliot's *Murder in the Cathedral* (1936). Then CBS took over and renamed it the CBS Radio Playhouse in 1936 and CBS Studio 50, a television studio, in 1950. The house was renamed the Ed Sullivan Theatre in 1967, to honor the man whose long-running TV variety show had emanated from the theatre since 1957.

2 Auditorium, Hammerstein's Theatre, 1927

Sullivan retired from broadcasting in 1974, but the house continued to be used by CBS, which refurbished it in 1993 for *The David Letterman Show*. The late-night comedian turned the theatre and its neighbors into something of a New York tourist attraction, visited by thousands of his fans.

1 The Broadway entrance to Hammerstein's Theatre, marked by a tall sign and standard marquee, was in a thirteen-story office building. A long corridor led to the auditorium, which had frontage on 53rd Street. This original drawing of the structure, prepared and signed by Herbert J. Krapp Architect, is a somewhat romantic representation of the buildings as they stand today.

2 Architect Herbert Krapp was able to indulge his lifelong passion for Gothic design in the plans for the interior of Hammerstein's Theatre. In many ways the auditorium bore more resemblance to a cathedral than to a theatre. The stage is flanked with large alcoves, each containing five backlit murals, painted by J. Scott Williams, with scenes from the operas Oscar Hammerstein had premiered in New York. Heraldic motifs fill similar arches in the balcony walls. Ribs coming up from the sides converge in a central dome. Between the ribs Krapp had the walls painted to resemble mosaic tilework in his familiar Adam arabesques.

Ethel Barrymore Theatre

243-49 West 47th Street

Herbert J. Krapp, Architect • Opened December 20, 1928; 1084 seats

The last of the twenty-one theatres the Shuberts built between 1908 and the 1929 Crash, the Ethel Barrymore was intended as a showcase for one of Broadway's premier actresses. But show business being what it is, the name Ethel was removed from the house signage when the Shuberts and the star parted company in 1932. Miss Barrymore had appeared in four none-too-well-received plays at the theatre. Other plays had some success, including *Death Takes a Holiday* (1929), Noel Coward's *Design for Living* (1933), and Clare Booth Luce's *The Women* (1936). The Barrymore was large enough to support musical comedies, including *The Gay Divorce* (1932), *Knickerbocker Holiday* (1938), *Pal Joey* (1940), and *Best Foot Forward* (1941). The theatre's first Pulitzer-Prize-

winning production was Tennessee Williams' *A Streetcar Named Desire* (1947); *Look Homeward, Angel* also won, in 1957. Other familiar names from this period are *Tea and Sympathy* (1953) and *A Raisin in the Sun* (1959). In the 1960s and '70s productions at the Barrymore generated little excitement, with the exceptions of the thriller *Wait Until Dark* (1966) and a now-forgotten musical with a sexual theme, *I Love My Wife* (1977), which ran for over two years. More recent shows have included David Rabe's *Hurly Burly* (1984), *Lettice and Lovage* (1990), for which British actresses Maggie Sullivan and Margaret Tyzack won Tony awards, Wendy Wasserstein's *The Sisters Rosenzweig* (1993; TRF Lincoln Center), and Zoe Wanamaker's stunning performance in *Electra* (1998).

1 The Barrymore's white brick facade has some terra-cotta trim but is dominated by a back-lit two-story blind arch above the twin bronze and glass canopies. (These were subsequently replaced by a standard Broadway theatre marquee.) The large terra-cotta grillwork screen is said to have been inspired by the public baths of ancient Rome. The stagehouse and its unsightly fire escapes are at the far right.

2 Entered from a shallow box office lobby, the auditorium of the Barrymore combines some Elizabethan and Mediterranean elements with the Adamesque plaster-work seen in most Shubert theatres. The principal decorative features were elaborate sunburst arch treatments arranged as concentric half-circles above the proscenium box entries. The intricate visual variety of this work has been obscured by subsequent repaintings.

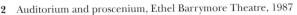

2 Auditorium and proscenium, Ethel Barrymore Theatre, 1987

Craig Theatre

152 West 54th Street & 145-57 West 53rd Street • R. E. Hall & Co., Architects

Opened December 24, 1928; 1434 seats • Reopened as Adelphi Theatre, November 27, 1934

The Craig Theatre, a purely speculative venture by an entrepreneur from Texas, was the last strictly legitimate theatre built in New York until the boom of the 1960s. The architects/builders had been responsible for a number of new theatres in the South during the 1920s. Characterized by actor William Gaxton as "the dump of all dumps," the Craig was home to flop after flop until it closed in 1931. Renamed for London's old Adelphi Theatre in 1934, the house languished until the WPA Federal Theatre Project moved in with a dramatization of Sinclair Lewis's *It Can't Happen Here* (1936). The Project also produced the *Living Newspaper*, dramatic presentations of contemporary events; *One Third of a Nation* (1938), an influential documentary on the U.S. housing problem; and a radical revue, *Sing for Your Supper* (1939). After the Project was closed, an esoteric religious group occupied the theatre until the Shuberts took it over. Their first booking was a hit, *On the Town* (1944), which soon moved to a better theatre, as did the Kurt Weill-Langston Hughes musical version of Elmer Rice's *Street Scene* (1947). The old Dumont Television Network used the theatre as a studio from 1948 until 1958, when it was reopened to legitimate use as the 54th Street Theatre. Two transfers, *Damn Yankees* (1958) and *Bye Bye Birdie*

2   Auditorium and proscenium, Craig Theatre, 1928

(1960), and two hits that transferred out, *No Strings* (1962) and *What Makes Sammy Run?* (1965), were the big successes. The house was renamed George Abbott Theatre, for the renowned theatrical genius, in 1965, but a string of flops soon convinced the Shuberts to sell the building. It was razed in 1970 to make way for the New York Hilton.

3   Box office lobby, Craig Theatre, 1928

1   The main entrance to the Craig Theatre was in a brownstone rowhouse that had been resurfaced to look even more nondescript than it had under its former owners. The auditorium and stagehouse were located in neighboring 53rd Street in a large warehouse-like structure.

2   The Craig's auditorium might easily have been mistaken for a high school assembly hall. It was finished in rough stucco with a minimal amount of limestone facing and Tudor-inspired paneling around the boxes and on the ceiling near the proscenium arch.

3   The virtually unadorned box office and entrance lobby extended through the renovated brownstone house into the auditorium.

Hollywood Theatre

1655 Broadway & 217-33 West 51st Street • Thomas Lamb, Architect

Opened April 22, 1930; 1506 seats • Reopened as Mark Hellinger Theatre, January 22, 1949

Like most of the movie palaces opened in New York City and around the country in the 1920s and '30s, the Hollywood was created as a glamorous setting for the fantasy world of the silver screen. The house was built by the Warner Brothers as a New York showcase for their new talking pictures. They also had the stage made large enough for live performances, and in 1934 opened a live revue, *Calling All Stars*, with Martha Raye. A George Abbott musical, *Sweet River* (1936), was among the other failures at the house, which was renamed 51st Street Theatre in 1940. Warners finally sold the building to a well-heeled producer, Anthony Brady Farrell, in 1948. He spent some more of his family money renovating the former movie palace, then renamed it for a prominent Broadway character, Mark Hellinger. Of five Farrell productions opened at the theatre, only *Texas Li'l Darling* (1949) managed to play more than 200 performances. Farrell had better luck when he switched from producer to landlord. *Two on the Aisle* (1951) and *Plain and Fancy* (1955) had respectable runs before the great *My Fair Lady* (1956) ran 2717 performances at the Hellinger. The 1960s and '70s were marked by such successful productions as *On a Clear Day You Can See Forever* (1965), Katharine Hepburn's musical debut in *Coco* (1969), *Jesus Christ Superstar* (1971), and the long-running *Sugar Babies* (1970). The Nederlander organization, which had bought the theatre in 1970, tried to find good bookings after *Sugar Babies* closed in 1982, but finally gave up and sold the property to the Times Square Church in 1991.

2 Auditorium, Hollywood Theatre, 1930

3 Lobby rotunda, Hollywood Theatre, 1985

1 The main entryway to the Hollywood Theatre occupied very little of the architects' attention. At the time it was desirable for a first-run motion picture theatre in Times Square to have an entrance, however small, on Broadway. These doorways were sealed off in 1934, and the main entrance was shifted around the corner to West 51st Street. There a large brick structure with a design based on an amalgam of modern influences still stands. The NRA banner in this vintage photograph proclaims the Warner Brothers' participation in the National Recovery Administration, a short-lived federal economic cooperation agency.

2 The rococo interior of the Hollywood/Hellinger is typical of 1920s movie palace design in the determination to impress through excess. The coved ceiling has dozens of murals reminiscent of Boucher and Watteau, depicting the 18th-century French aristocracy. A large plaster-of-Paris crown sits above the proscenium.

3 The spectacular lobby rotunda is dominated by eight fluted Corinthian columns and a ceiling that is decorated with colorful murals of classical scenes. This and other interior spaces were designed by Leif Neandross, chief designer of the Rambusch Decorating Studios.

163

RKO Roxy Theatre

1234-36 Sixth Avenue, 55-67 West 48th Street, 56-74 West 49th Street
Reinhart & Hofmeister; Corbett, Harrison & MacMurray; Hood & Foulihoux, Architects
Opened December 29, 1932; 3509 seats • Reopened as Center Theatre, September 22, 1934

Acclaimed by architectural critics, this Art Deco theater was demolished just 22 years after it was built as part of Rockefeller Center in 1932. The RKO Roxy, which became the Center Theatre after a lawsuit by the owners of the original Roxy Theatre just a block away, was planned as a film-and-stage-show house. However, its sister theatre, the larger and more spectacular Radio City Music Hall, took on this role in 1934 after failing as a venue for the revival of vaudeville. The RKO Roxy/Center began to book a variety of musical presentations, most with large casts and lavish sets. Shows included *The Great Waltz* (1934), a musical based on the lives of the Johann Strausses, father and son, and *The American Way* (1939), a disappointing epic by George S. Kaufman and Moss Hart. These and other offerings failed to strike the public fancy. In 1940, the Center managers, perhaps inspired by the popularity of the nearby Rockefeller Center ice skating rink, altered the stage to accommodate a show on ice. *The Ice Capades*, with many shows produced by the Olympic

2 Auditorium, toward house left, RKO Roxy Theatre, 1932

champion/movie star Sonja Henie, proved to be a hit attraction. After a decade of success, however, it became an economic imperative to melt the ice for the last time

1 The exterior of the Roxy Theatre was faced with the same Indiana limestone and bronze spandrels as the other Rockfeller Center buildings. At the time of the theatre's construction, Sixth Avenue was still dominated by the El that ran along most of its length. The plain facade with Art Deco signage stood in sharp contrast to its Old New York brownstone neighbors.

2 The walls of the theatre's auditorium were faced with mahogany veneer panels of two shades, and brass organ screens flanked the proscenium. On the ceiling, a large plaster chandelier was surrounded by a series of concentric circles decorated with the signs of the zodiac.

3 As in Radio City Music Hall, several elegant lounges occupied the lower level of the Roxy/Center. In the Gentlemen's Smoking Lounge photo murals by Edward Steichen depicted the early history of aviation. A similar note was struck in the Ladies' Lounge, with its back-lit frost-glass panel of Amelia Earhart's flight across the Atlantic.

3 Gentlemen's Smoking Lounge, RKO Roxy Theatre, 1932

and use the Center as a television production facility. Finally, in 1955, Rockefeller Center officials razed the magnificent showplace and replaced it with an office tower. Once again, an Art Deco showplace of the 1930s was replaced by a comparatively nondescript New York office building of the 1950s.

4   Auditorium, from stage, RKO Roxy Theatre, 1932

5   Auditorium, toward stage, RKO Roxy Theatre, 1932

4   The auditorium was vast, with its three balconies topped by a projection booth and other areas given over to technical uses. Because Rockefeller Center and its theatres were designed by a consortium of three architecture firms, it is difficult to assign responsibility for specific designs. There is no doubt, however, that the interior decorator Eugene Schoen played a major role in the original work on the RKO Roxy.

5   The auditorium walls were faced with panels of mahogany veneer of two shades, with brass organ screens flanking the proscenium. A pair of small side stages was used either as performance space or to display the theatre's two organ consoles. The handsome proscenium drape could be raised or lowered in a variety of contours.

Index

PICTURE CREDITS

Numbers refer to pages on which photos appear; A indicates photos at top of
page, B indicates those below.

MUSEUM OF THE CITY OF NEW YORK, Theatre Collection—1, 5, 6, 8, 16B,
18A, 19A, 20, 21, 22, 24, 32, 34, 43B, 46, 49B, 50A, 57A, 59A, 61, 62B, 64,
65A&B, 73, 84, 96, 140. Byron Collection—2, 3A&B, 4, 7, 10, 12, 14, 15, 17,
18B, 23, 25, 26, 28, 29, 30, 33, 35, 37A&B, 39, 44, 45, 97A&B. Wurts
Brothers Collection—11A&B, 71, 78, 79, 87A, 88, 90A, 91, 92A&B, 94, 130,
134.

NEW YORK HISTORICAL SOCIETY—27, 38, 40, 43A, 48, 54, 60, 66, 125,
126B, 127A&B, 139A, 164, 165B, 166A. NEW YORK CITY, Landmarks
Preservation Commission (Carl Forster photos)—83B, 87B, 114, 139B,
151B, 155B, 159, 163B. NEW YORK PUBLIC LIBRARY—13, 53A&B, 85,
144, 145B, 158, 162, 166B; White Studios Collection—74, 98, 99, 106, 107,
115, 152, 153A&B, 160, 161A&B.

SHUBERT ARCHIVE—59B, 68, 70A&B, 82, 116, 117, 118, 120, 121, 129.

UNIVERSITY OF TEXAS, Theatre Arts, Harry Ransom Humanities Research
Center—19B, 47, 55, 67B, 69, 75, 86, 93B, 95. WISCONSIN CENTER FOR
FILM AND THEATER RESEARCH—16A. B'HEND & KAUFMANN
ARCHIVES—122, 131, 133A, 136, 145A, 155A. HARVARD UNIVERSITY,
Theatre Collection—62A, 137. THEATRE HISTORICAL SOCIETY,
Chicago—41, 42B.

FOX & FOWLE—93A, 133B. HARDY HOLZMAN PFEIFFER ASSOCIATES—
119, 135A, 143. LIBRARY OF CONGRESS—63. NEW VICTORY THE-
ATRE, Elliott Kaufman photo—31. RAMBUSCH STUDIOS—163A. Mr
MARCY CHANIN—147A. PEGGY AND PETER ELSON— 100, 101A&B,
103, 105, 156-157. PEGGY ELSON—154. LIONEL FREEDMAN—57B.
MARK HYLTON—9. AUTHOR, private collection—36, 42A, 49A, 50B,
51, 52, 56, 58, 67A, 72A&B, 74, 76, 77A&B, 80, 81A&B, 83A, 89, 90B,
102, 104, 108, 109, 110-113 (White Studios), 123, 124A&B, 126A, 128,
132, 135B, 138, 141, 142, 146, 147B, 148, 149, 150, 151A, 165A.